No Plans
to Quit

TORN CURTAIN PUBLISHING
Auckland, New Zealand
www.torncurtainpublishing.com

ISBN Softcover 978-1-991299-52-9
ISBN ePub 978-1-991299-53-6

All details included in this book are written from the author's best recollection, available information or personal perspective. Names, stories and photographs of people mentioned in this book have been used with permission as much as possible. In any instance where the author has been unable to locate or contact the person to obtain permission, the author will be pleased to rectify this at the earliest opportunity.

Although the author and publisher have made every effort to ensure that the information in this book was correct at the time of press, the author and publisher do not assume and hereby disclaim any liability to any party for any loss, damage, or disruption caused by errors, inclusions or omissions, whether such errors, inclusions or omissions result from negligence, accident, bias or any other cause.

This book does not in any way represent the opinions or position of any organisation, institution or individual other than the author.

Unless otherwise noted, scripture references are the author's own paraphrase.

All scripture quotations marked CEV are from the Contemporary English Version® Copyright © 1995 American Bible Society. All rights reserved.

Scripture quotations marked GNT are from the Good News Translation® (Today's English Version, Second Edition) Copyright © 1992 American Bible Society. All rights reserved.

Scripture quotations marked NASB are taken from the New American Standard Bible®, Copyright © 1960, 1971, 1977, 1995, 2020 by The Lockman Foundation. Used by permission. All rights reserved. Lockman.org

All scripture quotations marked NIV are taken from the New International Version®, NIV®. Copyright © 1973, 1978, 1984, 2011 by Biblica, Inc.™ Used by permission of Zondervan. All rights reserved worldwide.

Scripture quotations marked NLT are taken from the Holy Bible, New Living Translation, copyright © 1996, 2004, 2015 by Tyndale House Foundation. Used by permission of Tyndale House Publishers, Inc., Carol Stream, Illinois 60188. All rights reserved.

Typeset in PT Serif and PT Sans.

Cataloguing in Publishing Data
Title: No Plans to Quit
Author: Trevor McKinlay
Subjects: Local Church History, Presbyterian Church of New Zealand, 150 Year Church Anniversary, Missions, Church Administration, Congregational Life, Cromwell New Zealand, Southland Otago, Christian Life and Ministry

A copy of this title is held at the National Library of New Zealand.

No Plans
to Quit

CROMWELL PRESBYTERIAN CHURCH
PASSES THE 150-YEAR MILESTONE

TREVOR McKINLAY

Foreword

CROMWELL AND DISTRICTS PRESBYTERIAN CHURCH (now widely known as Cromwell Presbyterian Church, or CPC) has a rich and engaging history. In my life as a Presbyterian minister, I've had many connections with people there. I trained with the Reverend David Caldwell (see Chapter 5 in this book), convened the Ministry Settlement Board which 'called' the Reverend Rob Pendreigh from Cromwell to Balclutha, and, latterly, it's been my privilege to serve as the Stated Supply Minister at Cromwell for 13 months in 2023-2024.

Parish history plays a vital role in portraying faith and life in the wider community; otherwise, local history can lack a deeper understanding of those communities and the people in them. Understanding faith in Otago, and in particular Central Otago, means understanding and reflecting on the life, witness and story of the Presbyterian Church.

Trevor McKinlay has done a splendid job in researching and writing CPC's story. It's both entertaining and illuminating. The parish started as a mission outreach and grew through difficult and challenging times. There are troubling controversies, inspiring acts of faithful Christian service, and stunning examples of life and growth, especially in building the present church complex.

Today, the church continues to grow and influence the wider community when many other Presbyterian churches have significantly reduced in size and impact, or closed. Why, one might ask, does CPC stand out as a spiritual light today? I am persuaded the Lord has a special future for the congregation there, at a time when many people live very secular lives and see little room for God.

My prayer is that CPC continues to thrive and inspire the wider denomination and the surrounding diverse Christian faith communities. I am sure the Sesquicentennial celebrations in February 2025 will be a delight for all who attend—and a springboard for challenging times ahead.

The Reverend Dr Tony Martin
January 2025

Contents

Introduction

THIS IS A STORY ABOUT ONE CENTRAL OTAGO church. It is not, however, written only for the people of this church, and certainly not only for church people in general. Nor should it be: the people of the Cromwell Presbyterian Church have always tried to be part of, and stay connected to, the wider local community.

This is a story for everyone ... it just isn't your average history. Yes, it does look at what's happened in the 150 years this Cromwell church has been around, and the main focus is the recent past— the last fifty years—because a Stated Supply Minister,[1] Robert Paterson, wrote a short but very readable history of the first one hundred years to coincide with the centennial celebrations in early 1975.

To connect with Robert Paterson's record, we'll start with an overview of those first one hundred years. However, some may be surprised to discover that the real focus of the book is the church as it is now, for as the years slip by, the 'now' of today will become the yesterday of tomorrow and beyond. With fewer people growing up through Sunday Schools and Bible Classes as in the past, it seems helpful to 'tell church like it is today' so that readers who have no church connection will at least know what it

---

1 Presbyterian term for a relief minister for a specified period.

is they're missing. This 'current' part of the story will offer many glimpses into the connections that exist between the church and the local community.

The book's post script is a look at the church of the future. It's written at a time when the world has very few certainties and has never had greater need. As I write,

- the world holds its breath to see what Donald Trump, the reactionary criminal but re-elected US President, does to the world after winning the White House again;
- the Ukraine war drags on;
- Israel pushes its jaw out defiantly at a world aghast at the thousands of innocent people who are dying in Gaza and Lebanon after the Hamas atrocities in October 2023;
- here at home, we're divided by race—and increasingly, by poverty.

If Christians are going to be much use in this world that is on the verge of tearing itself apart, they'll need to remind themselves of the example of Jesus—not the obscure stained-glass window fellow, but the flesh-and-blood bloke who lived as we have and who died in a way none of us would want to . . . and then changed history by coming back to life and showing us that He (Yep, capital H) is surely the Son of God, as the Roman centurion at the cross on the hill outside Jerusalem declared that first Easter.

So, Christians are:

- far from perfect, with the same mix of potential to be likeable and nasty as anyone else—just forgiven for the wrong things they've said and done;
- actively ashamed of deeds in any Christian institution that brings the name of Jesus or faith into disrepute, e.g. abuse of people in care;
- trying to be servant men and women, carers who seek the best for others;
- always up for a good time, so whether or not they use alcohol, they like that story about Jesus turning water into wine at a place called Cana in Galilee because of the joy, laughter and fun it portrays;
- last, but definitely not least, people who cling to the resurrection hope of life after death, however much that's been ridiculed by those who don't believe in God.

What Christians are not (or shouldn't be) is:

- part of a privileged few;
- head-in-the-sand 'ostriches' or 'refugees from real life', averse to having fun;
- apologetic about their faith;
- more likely to be cowardly, weak or timid than others;
- utterly self-centred;
- under-achievers content with doing as little as they can in the time given to them.

I hope this book makes you smile more than cringe! If you're not currently a person of faith, do consider starting out on the faith journey yourself, or at least discover why at Cromwell Presbyterian Church, there are no plans to quit.

Trevor McKinlay
January 2025

CHAPTER ONE

The First Fifty Years

CENTRAL OTAGO IS A HAUNTINGLY BEAUTIFUL BUT rugged part of New Zealand which, since the first settlers arrived in the late 1840s, has thrown challenges in front of all who have ventured here. After Hartley and Reilly's discovery of gold in 1862, just south of Cromwell,[2] men (and very few women) came from all over the world in search of this South Island treasure.

Picture them landing in droves from Australia, but also from Europe, the United States, and other faraway places—all eager to make their fortune. So many come from China that, just as in

---

2   American Horatio Hartley and Irishman Christopher Reilly deposited a bag of gold weighing just under 40 kg on the Treasury desk in Dunedin in August 1862. Diggers worked the river beaches of the Clutha, Kawarau and Shotover, and higher up in their tributaries. A lucky few made a packet. Many perished in heavy snowfalls and winter floods. In icy gorges, the sun never reached the floor and piles of wash froze cement hard. A diet of flour and tea meant that many developed scurvy. At the peak of the Otago rush in 1863 the goldfields population was estimated at 24,000. (https://teara.govt.nz/en/gold-and-gold-mining/page-3)

Gabriel's Gully a few years earlier,[3] the Chinese miners create a village of their own for mutual support and comfort. Honest and hard workers, they rarely complain or misbehave when things go badly. They usually work old, long-abandoned claims, which means finding gold is a tougher proposition for them. At times, with no money to buy rice, they boil wheat for their meals.

These are the days before double-glazing, wood burners, insulation, refrigeration and heat pumps. Apart from the harsh environment, Cromwell, tucked in the geographical heart of Central Otago, is a tough place to live. There aren't a lot of employment options. One can set up as a farrier, plumber, carpenter, or blacksmith, but paying customers aren't that numerous down here; the New Zealand 'fix-it-yourself with Number 8 wire' mentality surely has its beginnings in places and times such as this.

Still, the excitement of the gold rush persists in one form or another, as miners try panning by hand, sluicing, dredging the waterways, and quartz crushing until well after the turn of the century. Very few make their fortune; quite a lot find just enough gold to keep body and soul together—and to keep them looking for more. Many don't survive the rigours of Central Otago's winters, struggling to make enough money to keep warm, with unrecorded miner deaths potentially numbering in the thousands.

Little by little, the thrill of the gold rush subsides, and miners head off to seek their fortune in far-off places. Many, however, stay in this wild and beautiful land and make an attempt at an ordinary

---

3   Gabriel's Gully is 3km from the town of Lawrence near the Tuapeka River. Gold was found there by Gabriel Read on 25 May 1861, and this led to the Otago gold rush.

living. Life is still very basic, and communications are primitive. There are no roads at first—not even a beaten track until bullock drays and horse-and-cart combinations have travelled a route enough times to show the way. In the absence of bridges, punts and barges are used to cross the rushing Central Otago rivers. Sadly, there are drownings recorded where either a makeshift bridge or barge or even the travellers themselves in their attempt to ford a fast-flowing river, are swept away.

Railways emerge onto the scene in a period of serious economic downturn, and they are built in exceptionally difficult conditions.

> *The railway builders were an unbelievably tough bunch. A combination of labourers, stonemasons and blacksmiths worked digging tunnels, constructing complex viaducts, building culverts and laying lines through extremely difficult country . . . by and large the work was done by hand using only picks, shovels and wheelbarrows.*[4]

It takes twenty-nine years from the track's commencement in 1878, for the railhead to reach Clyde—and another fourteen years for passenger services to arrive in Cromwell.[5]

Amidst such hardships, church pioneers make their way into the goldfield settlements of the early 1860s. It is incredibly tough for them as they join the struggle to survive, whilst also preaching the Christian message. And there are plenty who don't care if these Christian pioneers are in difficulty.

---

4   Nicola McCloy, *Central Otago History in Bite-sized Chunks*, Flying Books Publishing, 2023, p.93

5   The railway from Dunedin to Cromwell. https://mightyclutha.blogspot.com

'Captain' Jackson Barry, a colourful entrepreneur and politician, is one of these early arrivals. Soon, he becomes the Mayor of Cromwell. Dr D M Stuart, one of the Presbyterian leaders in Otago and a revered minister of Knox Church, makes the long journey from Dunedin to Cromwell in the early 1860s, to chair a meeting about the establishment of a church in Cromwell. There, Barry uses his soapbox orator skills to persuade the people who want a church that this is a matter requiring prior consultation with all the townsfolk.[6]

Nevertheless, church services begin in Cromwell with various ministers travelling long distances on horseback—Rev Dr Copland from Lawrence, Rev Connor from Oamaru who comes via the Lindis Pass, and even, as mentioned, the renowned Dr Stuart from Dunedin. Other preachers come and go also, but in the late 1860s, the appointment of Rev C S Ross as minister at Clyde—a mere fifteen miles away through the Cromwell Gorge—brings real hope for those who still want to see a church formally established in Cromwell.

Ross unfortunately does not keep good health, but he nevertheless,

> ... made long journeys (through Central Otago) stimulating interest and organising to prepare the way for later ministerial settlements.[7]

---

6   Robert M Paterson, *100 years: the centennial of the establishment of the Parish of St. John, Presbyterian Church of N.Z., Cromwell, Lowburn, Bannockburn*, Cromwell Presbyterian Church, 1975, pp.1-2

7   John Collie, *The Story of the Otago Free Church Settlement*, Presbyterian Bookroom, NZ, 1949, pp.72 & 120

In November 1867, Ross officiates at the first Cromwell service held in the schoolhouse. More firsts follow in 1868, including the first celebration of Communion. Participants all drink from one large 'common cup' with the minister or other server wiping the rim after each person drinks—something that certainly wouldn't happen in later times! Fermented wine is used instead of the red cordial now served in many 21st-century churches. Ross also calls a public meeting, at which a Cromwell Church Committee is formed, and others soon follow in Bannockburn and Kawarau Gorge. The latter group meets in the Sluicers Arms Hotel, near the south-eastern end of the Kawarau Gorge, but this committee only lasts three years as miners eventually leave the district entirely.

In July 1868, the Rev Benjamin Drake arrives in Cromwell. A Congregational minister who has served in both England and Tasmania, Drake initially does relief preaching for various Presbyterian churches in Hokitika and Invercargill before applying to register as a Presbyterian minister, but the Otago and Southland Synod—the controlling body of a church and area—turns down his application. Instead, they recommend he work in several Presbyterian churches before re-applying. It takes numerous more applications spread over seven years, before, at last, Rev Benjamin Drake is inducted into the newly sanctioned Cromwell parish on 11 February 1875. He is sixty-five years of age.

Although Drake now ministers in the parish of Cromwell, he also serves the wider region in a relief capacity. This arrangement slows the growth of the church, by not making full use of an outstanding leader while he still has good years left to give. Drake has the enthusiastic endorsement of his parishioners and successive deputations of Synod who are sent to evaluate his work in Cromwell. Back in the 1850s, he was the tireless and very capable representative of workers exploited by landowners in Essex, England. He even arranged passage for around eight hundred such workers, who travelled in successive ships to Launceston, Tasmania, where the need for skilled labour was massive.[8]

While it seems fair that Free Presbyterians are careful about who ministers in their churches, it is a sad fact that—particularly in regards to a parish located on the opposite side of the world from their native Scotland—they would not allow these churches to select their own minister. In 1843, the Scottish church's refusal to give this freedom is one of the grievances that causes more than four hundred ministers to break away and create the 'Free Church'.[9]

Meanwhile, Drake carries on as the de facto minister of Cromwell for over six years before he's officially appointed. His new parish covers an area stretching eighty miles long by forty miles wide. There's no church building, no manse provided for Drake and his family, no Session or Deacons' Court. There *is*, however, a typhoid epidemic in 1872.[10] But Drake is up for this challenge too! Truly a man for all seasons, his capacity and capability are praised in these two reflections:

[Drake's] preaching is vigorous and memorable . . . delivered in blunt, straight sentences, with apt illustrations.

---

8   https://historyoverdinner.com/the-reverend-benjamin-drake/
9   Collie, op. cit. pp.4-5. Many of those on the first ships bringing immigrants to Port Chalmers in 1848 are 'Free Presbyterians'. pp. 14-15
10   Paterson, op. cit. pp.4-5

I often wonder if we've had many abler men since.[11]

Drake serves as minister until June 1878, then retires, remaining in Cromwell until his death in 1890. His passing is mourned by church folk and townspeople alike.

He was . . . a beloved pastor. Wherever he went, people welcomed him warmly, and in the lonely valleys they looked forward to his visits with great excitement.[12]

Local historian J C Parcell declares Drake's life to have been "one of the most generous ever spent in the service of mankind."[13] An obituary in the *Cromwell Argus* newspaper is even more eloquent:

Thus, at the ripe old age of eighty, departed from this world a man . . . beloved, honoured and respected by all . . . his kindly . . . ways, his sterling honesty and integrity, his genial manner to both young and old, his charitable and unselfish disposition, and above all, his earnest and diligent ministrations in the service of his Master, won for him a reverential regard so intense that in his declining years he came to be looked upon as the Patriarch of the district.[14]

Filling the vacancy Drake leaves upon his retirement proves tricky—a problem made all the more difficult as there isn't yet a church building. But by the time Drake departs this world, real progress is being made to rectify the situation. When the next appointee, Rev James Blackie, is inducted on 19 August 1880, a

---

11   Paterson, op. cit. p.4
12   Paterson, op. cit. p.4
13   J. C. Parcell, *Heart of the Desert*, Whitcombe and Tombs, 1951, p.347
14   Cromwell Argus Gazette, July 1890

church building is at last under construction, which is officially opened on 1 April 1881.

A single man from a farming background, the new reverend is the first of many for whom Cromwell will be their first ministry placement. Blackie is a man's man—an energetic, sleeves-rolled-up sort of person with a talent for music. Widely acclaimed for his violoncello playing, he is further rated highly as one of the first students to enter the Dunedin theological hall at Knox College.

> *[Blackie] spent over six years in this, his first charge . . . he proved a most inspiriting force, stirring up the congregation to vigorous activity and progress. He was deeply interested in the Chinese, of whom there were large numbers . . . would have gone to China if he could have.*[15]

Blackie offers excellent services to the Cromwell region, but sadly he retires from this role on 28 November 1886. His departure is marked by a strange incident that bemuses the local community:

> *A very strange incident concerning Mr Blackie's last day in Cromwell. His horse apparently judged by the bustle and excitement that something unusual was about to happen, and perhaps objected to leaving . . . for he quietly walked out of the gate, trotted down the road, and vanished into the distance . . . search and enquiry were fruitless. His master neither saw nor heard of him again.*[16]

---

15 Alexander Don, *Memories of the Golden Road: A History of The Presbyterian Church in Central Otago (Revised ed.)*, Published AH &AW Reed, Dunedin, 1936, p.325

16 Don, op. cit. p.180

Blackie goes to Lumsden, some ninety-five miles south of Cromwell, where he takes the role of minister in the huge parish of Taringatura. There, he toils long and hard for eleven years, only to die suddenly and much too young in 1897.

Back in Cromwell, the Reverends Blake, Connor, Ferguson and Hunter cover the vacancy left by Blackie, which lasts two years. On 3 October 1888, Hunter is officially inducted. The first occupant of a new cottage manse—for which Synod pays the full grant of three hundred pounds—Hunter is a passionate and fiery preacher, but something of a loner. People find him difficult to talk to, and he leaves after just two years. Another long vacancy stretches out for the church before Rev James Cumming, fresh from the University of Edinburgh, begins his ministry in Cromwell on 20 April 1892. He marries Miss McGrogan, a local teacher, further cementing himself as part of the local community. An able academic, Cumming is eventually appointed Professor of Old Testament at Knox and Moderator of the General Assembly—the annual gathering of Presbyterian leaders from all parishes across New Zealand.

By 1890, the economy is improving and there's growing local optimism with Cumming's appointment going so well. The church appoints its first elders (known as *Session*) in October 1892, and this new group proves very active. With Cumming acting as Chair, Session supervises elections for the church committees and forms a Deacons' Court for specific pastoral and management tasks. They even set up a Christian Endeavour Society in a joint initiative with the newly formed Methodist Church, long before churches are in the habit of sharing much of their work.

With most of these groups being traditionally the domain of men, it is a welcome initiative when Ladies' Guilds appear, supporting women in the church and making sure their viewpoints are heard. While the minister's wife often appears to live in her husband's shadow, she works tirelessly, providing hospitality, offering counsel to other women, and greeting the congregation with a welcoming smile. She is expected to be all things to all people.

The winds of change are just starting to blow in New Zealand. In September 1893, Governor Glasgow signs a new Electoral Act into law, propelling New Zealand into standing as the first self-governing country in the world to give women the vote in parliamentary elections. It will be almost twenty years before suffragettes take to the streets in the United Kingdom, demanding the same rights in 'The Home Country'.

In the realm of church politics, Cumming is personally opposed to 'Church Union'—a movement that unites the Free Churches south of the Waitaki River with all other Presbyterian churches in the country. His stance reflects the widespread caution of the Free Church people whose very presence in New Zealand was caused by the 1843 split in Scotland. So deep-seated is this division, that only in 1901 is there reconciliation between the Presbyterian Church of New Zealand and the Free Presbyterian Church of Otago and Southland.[17] Christians know well enough what the Bible says about sorting out their differences,[18] but it is fifty-three years after the first ships land at Port Chalmers—and

---

17 Collie, op. cit. pp.171-177

18 "My dear friends, as a follower of our Lord Jesus Christ, I beg you to get along with each other. Don't take sides. Always try to agree in what you think" (1 Cor. 1:10 CEV).

only after many long and sometimes acrimonious debates—that Church Union finally takes place. More than a century later, Southern Presbytery and Synod are still effectively in charge of all things Presbyterian, south of the Waitaki.[19]

Cumming eventually leaves Cromwell in 1898, and the church faces an unsettled time as three more ministers come and go in the lead-up to the First World War.

Cumming's successor, the Rev Thomas Tait, serves the church of Cromwell from 1899-1904, with his ministry spanning New Zealand's fight in the Boer War from 1899-1902. When, after a seven-month siege by the Boers, the South African town of Mafeking (now Mahikeng) is finally freed, Cromwell holds lively celebrations.

In February 1906, Rev J G McLeod takes over from Tait. An earnest and faithful preacher, he is plagued by ill-health which forces him to resign from the church in October 1908. While Cromwell awaits a new minister, the Bannockburn Church is opened on 7 March 1909. Unfortunately, McLeod dies suddenly in September 1910, leaving a widow and two small children, and Cromwell still without a minister. Less than six months later, McLeod is succeeded by Rev W P Rowlands who is inducted in February 1911. Rowlands is well-regarded, but he also lasts less than three years. Resigning unexpectedly in November 1913 due to 'urgent family reasons', he moves across to Melbourne in Australia.

It is not a good record for Cromwell. Collectively, the previous two ministers have served for a total of just five years and five months. The parish remains vacant for a further four years and

---

19 Local colloquialism for the Waitaki River.

two months. *Is there a more fundamental problem here?* But there is no time for reflection—just eight months after Rowlands leaves for Australia, World War One breaks out. A wave of patriotic anti-Kaiser sentiment brings momentary fervour to a struggling town, but soon the sombre shadow of war spreads across the whole country.

Two Wars and a Depression

ON 4 AUGUST 1914, WORLD WAR ONE BREAKS OUT. This is long before the advent of television, so the events precipitating the war can't be seen on a screen. Not that they would mean much anyway in faraway New Zealand, except that—just as with the Boer War from 1899-1902—where Great Britain goes, we go. Many New Zealanders in the early 1900s are migrants from the United Kingdom, and Britain will affectionately be called 'home' for many years to come. We're not independent yet; we're still part of the British Empire upon which, it is often boasted, the sun never sets. What Britain wants, we want too.

Cromwell men soon answer the call to arms, including many from Cromwell Presbyterian Church (CPC). The army wisely keeps local boys together in the Otago Division, and, as with the Boer War, there's plenty of patriotic sentiment around. A pamphlet popular in New Zealand at the time preached, "The genius of the British race is rooted in justice, truth, honour and consideration for the rights of others." Another reiterated the New Zealander's "double patriotism—that of his own country, and the wider patriotism of the great empire to which he is proud to belong."[20]

After W P Rowlands resigns and moves to Australia in late 1913, Cromwell Presbyterian Church is taken up by Rev W P Rankin. Already a Stated Supply Minister, he is officially inducted in November 1914. Five months later, New Zealand is a key part of an invasion force fighting the Turks at Gallipoli. Rankin is prominent in patriotic activities. He works hard, both to rally support for the troops and to keep up morale in the hometown they have left behind.

In this district, he will remain long in memory because of his patriotic concerts given during World War One, when the whole town and countryside could always be relied upon to turn out to hear him sing 'Mother Machree', 'Dona' and many other favourites. He took much more than a passing interest in the town's affairs and willingly gave his time and energies to all worthy causes.[21]

Along with his active engagement and heartfelt input into the town of Cromwell, Rankin also involves himself in golf and bowls. He is respected, even loved, and becomes the longest-serving minister in the church's history.

War always casts a shadow over the participating countries, and it is hard to imagine a 'winner' when World War One finally

---

20 Michael King, *Penguin History of New Zealand*, Penguin, 2003. p.293

21 J. C. Parcell, *Heart of the Desert*, Whitcombe and Tombs, 1951

comes to an end in 1919. The human price—paid in senseless slaughter in the trenches of Gallipoli and the Western Front—has been high for all countries involved.

Thirteen communicants of the Cromwell Church die in World War One. Captain William Jolly—a prominent leader in both church and community, as was his father D A Jolly before him—is killed at Armentieres[22], on the border between France and Belgium, in 1916. While en route to the Western Front, he had written several times to the children of the Cromwell Sunday School, telling them about the places he was visiting that are mentioned in the Bible: Sinai, the Red Sea, and Mary's Well.[23]

Another key member of the Cromwell community, Mrs Christina Foster—whose service as a Sunday School teacher lasts almost half a century—must endure receiving three telegrams informing her that each of her three sons has died. In 1949, Mr Gately will craft a memorial tablet from native wood, in the form of an open book, which will be placed in the foyer of the church as a memorial to those who have died in World War I and in the Second World War which followed twenty years later.[24]

Apart from their unspeakable sadness over the deaths of their beloved local men, the war is unsettling for Cromwell. As soldiers across New Zealand leave to face battle far across the seas, townsfolk begin drifting away from Cromwell as well, with some taking up vacancies elsewhere, or perhaps supporting wives and families who are struggling without male support. It's

---

22   According to church records.

23   One of the stained-glass windows in the Lowburn Chapel commemorates Captain Jolly.

24   It has pride of place in 2024, as it had in the original church, adjacent to the main door of the church.

not surprising, therefore, that three new elders—appointed only recently in 1913—shift from the district during the war or soon after it. R L Blair, an elder since 1910, also decides to relocate, and once again Cromwell Church's leadership resources are very thin. Robert Ritchie stays on as the sole elder—a position he'd also found himself in back in 1909—and he remains so until 1931.

As WWI ends, thousands of New Zealand men return home physically and mentally scarred. At the same time, the flu epidemic which is sweeping the globe finds its way to New Zealand shores, killing thousands.[25] Influenza takes almost half as many Kiwis as The Great War itself. Cromwell is fortunate to lose only four lives to the terrifying illness, but nearly nine thousand die nationwide. As the 1920s roll in, the economy is in a post-war, post-plague downturn, verging on an outright Depression. Morale can't have been lower too many times in our national history.

World War One leaves most economies very fragile, and New Zealand is no exception. The cost of rebuilding isn't often considered when countries decide to go to war. Unemployment in the early 1920s is high, and many struggle financially. It's hard to believe things are about to get much worse—as they do in the Great Depression of 1929-1935—before they'll start getting better, and it's no surprise that CPC's finances are also fragile. In 1926, when Rankin's long and meritorious service as minister comes to an end, the church is placed on Synod's Sustentation Fund, and the appointment of a minister to replace Rankin passes into the hands of Synod's Supply and Appointments Committee.

---

25   No one can be certain about how the Spanish flu virus reached New Zealand. Possibly on the liner Niagara or on returning troopships.

SUCH AN ARRANGEMENT BY THE REGIONAL Presbyterian authorities is hard for the Cromwell Church community to take. Cromwell is a long way from Dunedin, where the seat of power is, and there's often no personal connection with decision-makers. Besides, fending for yourself is a way of life in Central Otago. 'Independent' is not the same thing as 'stubborn and wilful'.

At this moment, the future looks bleak; such 'calls'[26] are for a minimum period of three years; if money stays tight, the appointment might lapse when the three years is up. But things turn out OK: both ministers, Chisholm (1926-32) and Heggie (1932-36) have their contracts extended, and the gap between them in 1932 is only four months. The Supply and Appointments Committee has acted promptly and positively and thus has not only helped with the money but ensured that there's continuity at a time when CPC couldn't have achieved that under its own steam.

While he may or may not be able to ride a horse, Chisholm (1926-32) is the first minister who comes with a car. This progress comes at a price: the car can't make it up the steep road to the Nevis, and before long, services there cease. On the plus side, services begin in the Ripponvale Hall and are well-supported.

Diamond Jubilee celebrations are held over 11-13 October 1930. It's fifty years since the Cromwell Church building opened in 1881. This momentous milestone brings about happy reunions and a sense of satisfaction with the church's overall progress.

---

26 Another term for 'appointment' within a church or ministry context.

But life is still very tough for most of Central Otago, especially those at the bottom of the income scale. As the Depression bites hard around 1932-1933, the church knows it must increase help where it can.

> *The new minister, Heggie, is called upon to undertake a great deal of Social Service work among the men in the camps established in the district for the relief of unemployment.*[27]

Signs of strain appear towards the end of Heggie's time as minister, but curiously, the situation doesn't catch the attention of respected Presbyterian authors Don or Collie in their otherwise impressive histories. The tension that taints Heggie's time in Cromwell mostly relates to the building of the Lowburn Church and, no doubt, the strain of serving the entire district in Depression conditions for four years.

> *Reports and discussions at the 1936 AGM were markedly different in tone from those of previous years . . . Some members had left the district, others had resigned from the church, the choir and much of the youth work had lapsed, finance had gone back, and various speakers commented on the unsatisfactory state of affairs.*[28]

Despite these dire observations, Heggie's work is praised after he departs for Roxburgh in 1936. It must be hard for him to leave things in such disarray, but his service is vigorously defended and praised:

---

27 Don, op. cit. p.341
28 Paterson, op. cit. p.18

Mr Heggie's ministry had been successful in many ways. His pulpit ministrations were of a very high order and congregations kept increasing, especially in the evenings. He always remembered too to visit the sick and the suffering.[29]

The ministry of George Renwick, another Scot, begins in December 1936 and lasts until November 1944. Not long after Renwick's appointment, Lowburn Church—the building venture which gave Heggie no small stress—is opened in April 1939. But there is more upheaval in store for the region.

The Great War (WWI) has not turned out to be 'the war to end all wars', despite some claims to this effect. Anger in Germany over what is seen as harsh and restrictive treatment by the Allies is one of the factors leading to support for Hitler. His Nazi party comes to power in the early 1930s, pushing the globe into World War Two in September 1939.

Despite the arrival of a fresh church minister, there's an unsettled air over Central Otago again, and for much the same reasons as plagued them in World War One: Allied troops are now caught up in World War Two, good men from the parish are being killed overseas, and families are moving elsewhere for various personal reasons.

After a 'considerable amount of negotiation', the Cromwell and Arrowtown parishes are amalgamated, mainly to rationalise expense and ensure ministry carries on in several locations.[30] The obvious advantage to both parishes is that they can share

---

29   Paterson, op. cit. p.18

30   In their book *Mountain Parish 1867-1990*, self-published 1990, D. G. & J. S. Jardine note rather tersely that the amalgamation with Cromwell is 'temporary'. It lasts for 46 years.

a minister and be self-sustaining, with the plan being outlined as follows:

> *The arrangement was for Cromwell and Arrowtown to each have one service every Sunday, and for Crown Terrace, Gibbston, Lowburn, and Bannockburn to have monthly services, sometimes on weeknights. Ripponvale churchgoers were brought into Cromwell by bus.*[31]

The flaw in this otherwise sensible arrangement is the increased cost—both in travel expenses and, perhaps more significantly, in the time and energy of the minister. Never an ideal arrangement for either district and requiring an 84-kilometre round trip for preachers, it is only in 1986 that Arrowtown is permitted its own minister again.

After Renwick, there's a long vacancy of fifteen months before Rev J C Doig becomes minister in February 1946. He comes from the West Coast, so he's used to isolation. He's also recently married. He stays in Cromwell until 1951, before moving down to Bluff. During Doig's time in the parish, Session is non-effective and rarely meets again during the next twelve years. Imagine a school of any size running with just the principal but no classroom teachers or volunteer parents in support! Where are the willing hands?

The years 1946 to 1957 feel quite flat for the combined Cromwell-Arrowtown parish. Is it just post-war and post-Depression fatigue? Is the 'double parish' too big a task for just one minister? When Doig leaves in 1951, he is replaced by the Rev Ian MacMillan—a 'quiet, sensitive man with real abilities'. MacMillan is a continuity

---

31   Paterson, op. cit. p.21-22

man, rather than a mover and a shaker, which suits this time when no one is crying out for innovation.

This strange flatness of church life in the decade following WWII may indeed contribute to the three-year vacancy after MacMillan—the longest empty stretch in CPC's one hundred and fifty-year life. It is described as:

> ... *perhaps the most trying in the whole history of the parish.*
> *A succession of students from the Theological Hall travelled*
> *to Cromwell by bus—four hours each way in those days—to*
> *take the services.*[32]

In sharp contrast with the drudgery that has become the Cromwell Church, national and world events are full of action and bring real cause for concern:

- The Cold War reaches its height in Europe.
- The 1950-1953 Korean War draws New Zealanders to fight under our country's flag for the fourth time in half a century.
- The 1951 waterfront strike sets Kiwi against Kiwi, 'haves' against 'have-nots'.
- The Tangiwai rail disaster in December 1953 saddens us all beyond words.
- We rush to contain the polio epidemic of the mid-1950s.

---

32 Including Paterson himself. The bus from Dunedin must have taken at least six hours each way. In 2025, it takes five hours on much-improved roads.

Even though Cromwell is so far removed from most of these happenings, they further heighten the sense of hopelessness and doom that seems to hover like a grey cloud.

There are times in our lives when the way forward is anything but clear, and we become frustrated because we can't get things going. That happens to churches sometimes, too. And that's when Christians learn to trust that God is still in charge. He gives us sufficient grace to carry on and somehow come out the other side of the gloom and uncertainty, stronger—or at least wiser—for the experience.

CHAPTER THREE

A Settled Season

BY THE EARLY 1970S, THE POPULATION OF CROMWELL is still less than one thousand. It's stable, like the town itself, with things carrying on much the same for thirty years after World War Two ends in August 1945. The country as a whole doesn't change a great deal, either. Two World Wars and a Depression have been enough for New Zealanders, thank you very much, and most South Island communities slip into a quiet and somewhat traditional way of life. Michael King observes that:

> *The public at large . . . mostly valued conformity and predictability in the behaviour of fellow citizens. Clothes of the day tended to be drab by previous and later standards, and short-back-and-sides haircuts were part of the national male uniform, while rugby, racing and beer did represent for most men the extent of recreational options.*[33]

33 King, op. cit. p.431

Economically, the country is getting stronger, with post-war commodity prices favouring meat, wool and dairy—New Zealand's prime exports. Apart from the waterfront strike in 1951, things feel settled enough. Even whiplash changes in government—with citizens pulling away from National in 1957, then coming straight back to the party in 1960—have little effect on daily life in Cromwell.

However, to refer to the 1960s version of Cromwell as 'a sleepy hollow' would puzzle or even irritate the residents of the day. Although it lacks the lively entertainment and various eating-out options of larger towns, it is orderly and clean—and the people here like it that way. Cromwell is a 'ribbon development,' with nearly all shops and businesses located on the main street that runs through the middle of the town. Most establishments stay open late on Fridays, but they still close for an hour in the early evening so that owners and employees can go home for dinner.[34]

Cromwell's three pubs are unimaginatively but affectionately known as the Top, the Middle, and the Bottom, reflecting their position on Main Road which slopes west to east down towards the river. Until the law changes in 1967, it's an open secret that pubs sell plenty of beer after closing hours. But even after the new closing time of ten o'clock comes into law, it only means the blinds will be drawn at 10 pm—you just have to know the door by which to enter and leave.

Church life reflects town life in its sense of decorum and order—most folks down here like it that way. There are just

---

34 This practice ceases quickly as the Clyde workforce builds up.

three churches now: Anglican, Catholic and Presbyterian.[35] Demonstrative, off-the-wall, unrestrained joy in church won't arrive until a Pentecostal church is set up in the 1980s.[36]

Since its opening in early 1881, Cromwell Presbyterian Church has been tucked in Inniscort Street, just up the hill from the bridge at the southeast end of town. Every Sunday morning the bells ring, calling churchgoers to gather; the bells also remind the rest of the town that Sunday is the day for church, whether you're planning to go or not. Inside, everything is in its place, with services running just as smoothly. A choir parades in at the beginning of the session and out at the end, with singers wearing bright red robes from neck to ankle.[37] Dress isn't rigidly formal, but some of the older folk still dress more formally with the men in suits or at least a collar and tie.

After its record three-year vacancy, Cromwell welcomes the Rev D A Calvert in February 1957. 'Marked advances' are noted under his ministry,[38] and despite money being tight, a real sense of togetherness is gained from church people providing voluntary labour for work on church buildings and toiling long and hard to cut and sell firewood. More importantly, the youth work of the church is boosted, with membership as strong as at any other

---

35 In 1891, stonemason Leslie Arthur builds the Methodist Church at the corner of Donegal and Erris Streets. His great-granddaughter, Helen Clark, is NZ's 37th Prime Minister (1999-2008). The Methodists close their church in 1960. The building will later become 'Arthur's', a very informal community movie theatre, until defeated by home movie options like Netflix and, perhaps, cold Cromwell winters.

36 Rev David Caldwell is the first minister to bring informal worship habits to Cromwell Presbyterian Church, and he begins his tenure in early 1984.

37 A generous donation by Mrs D Reid (Gibbston) enables the purchase of choir robes for the two churches.

38 Jardine, op. cit. p.94

time—the church choir is almost entirely Bible Class[39] participants. The church begins to host regular camps, and a parish newsletter is set up which immediately improves communications. Five new elders are appointed in 1958,[40] and Session is up and running again after a dry spell of almost a decade.

In 1964, the hard-working Calvert is succeeded by Rev W R Vinten who hails directly from Knox. Bigger news in town, however, is that local Cromwell boy Donnie Clark is playing for the All Blacks against Australia. He'll be followed in 1973 by another Cromwell lad, Lin Colling.[41] 'High priests' of the 'national religion' are always idolised here in Otago, and the little town of Cromwell is justly proud of its contributing talent.

The much-publicised 1967 trial of Professor Lloyd Geering, accused of heresy and 'disturbing the peace',[42] causes little reaction in Cromwell. There's not even a reference to it in Paterson's written history covering the years 1881-1981. Most country churches have a rather accepting faith, despite it not often being articulated. Doubts and questions may arise from time to time, but mostly these reflect the believers' frailty, rather than the authenticity of the Jesus story.

Rev Vinten is as energetic and well-regarded as his predecessor, but four years later, in 1969, he leaves for Wainuiomata in the

---

39 The equivalent of today's 'youth group'.

40 Paterson op. cit. pp.23-25

41 Lin Colling's brothers, Don and John, also played for Otago. Between them, the three brothers played 214 games for Otago and Don was captain from 1973-78. Community-minded but not otherwise connected to the Cromwell Church, Don is one of the three builders who led the way in the building of the new church in 2006.

42 The Geering Trial, with charges of heresy and disturbing the peace of the church, takes place before the General Assembly of the Presbyterian Church, November 1967. The fallout continues to this day.

North Island. Rev Neil Lambie, a likeable and outgoing man, follows Vinten, and the only objection is the shortness of his tenure—he's the fourth minister since 1906 to last three years or less, serving from 1970-1973.[43] Lambie goes on to become the chaplain at Scots College, an independent Presbyterian college in Wellington.

Outsiders can be forgiven for thinking the Presbyterian voice has too often been found missing when it comes to issues of social conscience. That is less likely from now on, with the first ripples of social unrest appearing on New Zealand waters in the 1960s. Fighting Hitler and the Japanese in WWII was the right thing to do, but the reasons for the war now taking place in Vietnam aren't so clear. Although CPC itself does not seem to hold a collective position on Vietnam, for the first time in New Zealand's history, there's a strong objection nationwide to the government's decision to send forces to an overseas conflict. Protesters are present in considerable numbers when President Lyndon Johnson makes his whirlwind visit to New Zealand in October 1966.

Compulsory military training continues regardless. If your birthday comes up in the monthly ballot, not only must you attend an annual training camp for the next three years, your employer must give you leave to do it.[44]

Meanwhile, All Black rugby is facing the challenges caused by South Africa's apartheid era. Several All Blacks refuse to play the

---

43   Ministers three years or less at CMW: McLeod 1906-08; Rowlands 1911-13; MacMillan 1951-53, Lambie 1970-73.

44   Compulsory military training (CMT), a form of conscription, began in 1909 and finished in 1976. From 1961 onwards, those selected were required to complete three months' initial full-time training, followed by an annual commitment of three weeks of part-time training for three years.

Springboks in 1960, 1970 and 1976, and several more withdraw in 1981, including Graham Mourie, the All Black's captain of the previous year.[45] Things heat up in 1981 when the Muldoon Government allows a Springboks team to tour New Zealand—despite South Africa still being under apartheid and still refusing to consider black and coloured players for selection on sports teams.

The tour becomes a huge issue, even in Cromwell: the Otago Daily Times of Saturday 28 March 1981, gives prominence to Cromwell College teacher-coaches, including one from CPC, who decline to coach teams for competition games run by the NZ Rugby Football Union. Sports-loving Cromwellians don't hesitate to let the coaches know of their displeasure.

However, there is another situation that affects Cromwell far more directly than the South African rugby team's tour. In the early 1970s, the two major political parties had begun debating hydro-electric development in the Upper Clutha Basin and Cromwell Gorge. By 1975, drastic changes are afoot, including talk of a string of four dams being built on the Clutha and Kawarau Rivers.[46] Once the smoke of the political in-fighting clears after the 1975 election, the proposal of four dams has shifted into one

---

45 All Blacks who oppose playing South Africa until apartheid is over include Ken Gray, Chris Laidlaw, Bruce Robertson, and Graham Mourie.

46 In the 1970s, Schemes F and H are the most favoured options of the Clutha Valley Development proposals. Both advocate two developments on the Clutha River, with dams at Luggate and Queensberry. The difference is in the Cromwell Gorge, where Scheme F proposes one high dam at Clyde, and Scheme H proposes two lower dams in the Gorge. The effects of both on and up-stream of Cromwell would've been the same. Scheme H with the low dams would've had less impact on the orchards in the Cromwell Gorge. In 1976, the Government of the day decides to proceed with Scheme F; it considers this provides a greater power potential at a lower construction cost per unit of electricity.

large dam in Clyde, twenty-three kilometres south of Cromwell via the Cromwell Gorge. The implications for Cromwell are massive. A huge workforce will be required, the town will triple in size, and services will need to be ensured for all the new houses to be built. Add the increased demand for schooling, medical care, vehicle servicing, recreation, entertainment, and more, and the scope of this one project takes on staggering proportions.

In the second half of the 1970s, the reshaping of Cromwell is well under way, and by the time the Clyde Dam is completed and filled with water in 1993, hundreds of jobs will have been created. Cromwell becomes 'Construction HQ', with good money being earned and spent in the town. The resulting 'multiplier effect' grows the town as new businesses spring up everywhere. New arrivals move to the region for work, becoming service providers such as mechanics, surveyors, medical personnel, school staff and much more. A large supermarket replaces the friendly but much too small 4-Square store, and more banks arrive on the scene to set up in the new mall which opened in 1985.

Cherry growing for export largely replaces the fruit species previously grown for local and nationwide markets. A number of the newer folk at Cromwell Presbyterian Church are also local fruit growers. Allan and Sandra Perks come from Dunedin in the early 1960s, taking over a busy orchard that provides income for many. Their neighbours, Bill and Helen Irwin, previously toiled hard on a farm in the northern area of Southland, but they too grow fruit in Ripponvale. Their orchard is an adjunct to their professional lives, which also brings new skills and expertise into the region—Bill co-owns an engineering business, while Helen's skills as a teacher win her a senior manager role at the new Cromwell College in 1978. There are others, like John and Ann-Marie Leyser, Chris and Cherry McElligott, Bill and Joyce Darling, who all eke out a living from fruit, working hard for every cent and risking adverse weather events every year.

The improving science of grape growing soon reveals that Upper Clutha Valley is a prime vineyard area, with the soil boasting the ideal pH factor. By the dawn of the new millennium, the local pinot noir is much sought-after. Today, millions of dollars worth of wine is exported from Upper Clutha annually.

Sports facilities in the area also improve during this economic boom. What was a nine-hole golf course until the early 1970s, becomes a first-class eighteen-hole layout, annually hosting the final qualifying round for the New Zealand Golf Open. The Highlands Motor Sport Park alone has injected almost thirty million dollars into the community by using local contractors to construct their superb facilities. Anderson Park offers team sports opportunities in both summer and winter. The swimming pool is a welcome replacement for the ageing outdoor pool at the southeast end of town. There is even a squash complex, and the new Cromwell College soon adds tennis courts and a gymnasium to the town's sports facilities.

As these years of rapid development for Cromwell begin, Rev Doug Stout is the right man for the church. He arrives in 1976 with an absolute commitment to looking after the needs of people within his orbit—whether they are Presbyterians or not.

CHAPTER FOUR

Stout by Name, Stout of Heart

REV LAWRENCE DOUGLAS STOUT REMAINS SINGLE all his life. Those with family responsibilities might say it's easier for single people to give big chunks of their lives in service of others. We should recognise, however, that society needs all of us to give decent chunks of our lives in community service—be it through a church or in the wider community outside—whether we're married or single.

You never hear Doug talk about himself. During his ministry in Cromwell, no one recalls him mentioning two separate bombings of his hometown in the Shetland Islands in Scotland's far north— but he's there all right, aged just nine when some of his neighbours are killed in the 1941-1942 attacks. A plaque installed at Fair Isle South Lighthouse tells the story:

NO PLANS TO QUIT

During an air attack in December 1941, Mrs Catherine Sutherland, aged 22, the wife of an assistant lighthouse keeper, was killed and her infant daughter slightly hurt. On the 21st January 1942, during a second attack, a bomb hit the west end of the main block of houses. The building caught fire and was burnt out. The wife of the principal lighthouse keeper, Margaret Eileen Smith (60) and their daughter Margaret (Greta) Smith (10) were killed. William Morris (27) a soldier manning an anti-aircraft gun nearby, was also killed. Extensive damage was done by fuel, blast and flying debris.

Doug migrates to Nelson, New Zealand in 1959, then moves to Wellington where he works as an accountant for several years before receiving the call to become a minister. He trains at Knox College in Dunedin from 1967-1969, before heading to his first parish in Kurow, North Otago. Here, as well as his church duties, he's often seen in boots and overalls when extra help is needed.[47] As 1975 draws to a close, he moves again, this time down to Cromwell. His gift of looking after people's needs—not only in his church but also in the community at large—proves to be stunningly good. Selflessness personified. The town even names a street after him—Stout Terrace on the north-eastern side of town, which looks out to the Clutha River.[48]

In the mid-1970s, Cromwell and Districts Presbyterian Church is a typical rural parish, stretching forty-two kilometres northwest to Arrowtown, six kilometres north to Lowburn, and

---

47   PCANZ 1996 Assembly Memorial Minutes
48   Stout Terrace

seven kilometres southwest to Bannockburn. Sunday services take some organising—even the most willing of ministers can't be expected to take services in all three locations on the same day, *plus* the usual service at Cromwell. People must be found to ring the bells, greeters are required at the door, someone needs to play the piano or organ . . . More urgent than all of that, people reach out to the minister himself, seeking wise counsel for their concerns and problems, which are as real and urgent as they are anywhere in past times or today.

Bannockburn Church—which is sold twenty-five years later—is still running during Doug's eight years as minister. His Sunday duties begin at 9:30 am in Cromwell, then it's shared morning tea at the manse. At 10:45 am, the tea drinkers and sponge-cake scoffers are left to clean up while Doug jumps in his car and races out to Bannockburn for their 11 am service.

Doug is a good listener and a warm-hearted carer for anyone in need. You don't have to be a card-carrying Presbyterian for him to offer help or a kind ear. Cathy arrives in Cromwell in the late 1970s, a somewhat troubled young woman. Life is difficult for her. One night, in the small hours of the morning, she makes her way to the church, which she knows is never locked, seeking a space of sanctuary and comfort. Doug is a light sleeper, and he sits up in bed when he hears a noise from the church next door. He peers out the window of the manse to see a light on in the church, so he puts on his slippers and dressing gown and heads next door. He quickly recognises the somewhat distressed young woman inside the church. "Oh," says Doug without hesitation, "Let's go over to the manse and have a cup of Milo."

And they do. A few years later, Doug officiates at the wedding of Cathy and Chris Mann. In fact, for some considerable time after Doug has left Cromwell to take up a call in East Gore, young people in Cromwell will be asking him to officiate at their weddings. This happens so often that the Cromwell leadership eventually feels obliged to gently but firmly tell him to desist.[49]

Cathy becomes a rock of the church, a key member of the youth group leadership team, and a frequent visitor to a local rest home where, amongst other things, she keeps up the spirits of the residents by reading the Otago Daily Times out loud to those whose sight is failing. She never forgets Doug's gentle and open welcome towards a struggling young woman in the middle of the night. (Cathy's passing just before the publication of this book causes widespread sadness).

Yes, Doug is generous to a fault. When his car is stolen, Doug declares, "Oh well, he must have needed it more than I do." Of course, that's a bit naïve or at least impractical—he certainly does need his car to get around the parish—but Doug is a committed 'man for others', to an extent which many simply could not go. He doesn't just talk about God in church—he lives out his faith. And people love him for it.

> No manse could have been more fully open, nor hospitality
> so readily given, nor holidays so seldom taken.[50]

One Sunday, after a particularly heavy week of caring for his flock, Doug doesn't have a sermon ready. Instead, he takes a framed picture off the wall in the manse and marches it under

---

49 Session Minutes (p.125) for meeting 19 November 1991. General business, Item 3
50 PCANZ 1996 Assembly Memorial Minute

one arm into church. He declares he hasn't had time to prepare a sermon, and he then launches into an animated and off-the-cuff explanation as to what we can learn from this one picture.

He doesn't need to be forgiven for the lack of a sermon; after the service, more than one person is heard to say—amidst the general hilarity over the novelty of the message that day—that Doug's oration regarding the picture is up there with his best sermons anyway.[51] Sitting unspoken behind that truth is a bigger one: Doug Stout's service to Cromwell is so much more eloquent than mere words.

In his leisure time, such as it is, Doug serves as a leader in the Masonic Lodge. This will be more than a touch controversial for some evangelicals in future days, even verging on outrageous conduct for a minister. But in the rural South Island of the 1970s, only a few eyebrows are raised. At the time, there is no equivalent men's group in the Cromwell Presbyterian Church, and besides, is it not a good thing for churchmen to be rubbing shoulders with those in the wider community? Doug and other CPC men appreciate and contribute to the warmth of fellowship offered in the Lodge.

Across the road from Doug, Bill and Noreen How-John reside in their modest home. They're more than happy to keep an eye on the manse when the minister isn't there, and from time to time they help with practical, less 'men of the cloth' type tasks, such as starting lawnmowers.[52] Bill and Noreen own a much-loved cat,

---

51   This is an eyewitness account: the author is present when this happens.

52   One Saturday, Rev Robert Paterson, author of the 100-year history of CPC (1975) and relieving ('stated supply') minister at that time, asks to borrow a lawnmower. Even generous-spirited Bill hesitates because he can see three lawnmowers on the manse lawn already.

but the little animal soon discovers it will be gloriously spoiled if it turns up at the manse when Doug is in. Soon, it doesn't come home to Bill and Noreen's at all. Now and again they make an attempt to retrieve it, but the cat is a master of his own fate, and when the time comes for Doug to leave Cromwell, the cat mysteriously disappears too. A few months later, on a return visit to Cromwell, Doug pops around to let Bill and Noreen know that the cat is doing very well in Gore.

Doug's ministry in Cromwell coincides with the first eight years of the hydro-electric dam construction in Clyde. Huge changes take place within the congregation as the influx from the dam project brings people from many diverse backgrounds into the community: Church of Christ, Salvation Army, Brethren, and Baptist. The locals view such imports with a degree of caution and perhaps even suspicion, especially when a pew is removed from the back of the church to make room for little ones to play during the services while their parents supervise from adjacent seats. "Where have dignity and reverence gone?" some ask. But gradually, assisted by an amenable and open Rev Doug welcoming everyone from the front, the old guard relaxes into this new arrangement. It's refreshing having children around, and Doug quotes the words of Jesus:

> Let the little children come to me, and do not hinder them,
> for the kingdom of heaven belongs to such as these.
> *Matthew 19:14 NIV*

Home groups begin popping up, with some of the newcomers being accustomed to churches where, during the week, people get together in groups to study the Bible and provide each other with fellowship and mutual support. There's also a surge in music, and the choir's numbers increase, with Connie Perriam doing a fine job on the organ. New songs are introduced, led by two superb musicians in Janeice and Murray Robertson, and with more children and young people to draw from, Christian musicals are performed for the community by the church. In 1978, *The Jesus Story*, a children's musical with a Christmas theme, is produced by Rosalind Cox and directed by Trevor McKinlay. In April 1981, Trevor directs the new Cromwell College's first musical, *Joseph and the Amazing Technicolour Dreamcoat.* All the performances in the Town Hall are packed out.

Just as in other small country towns, teenagers are often left wanting for entertainment on the weekends. As more new families arrive, team sports at the college improve and become more numerous, but where and how to socialise is still a nagging question. With Murray Brown as the continuity person, various men soon put their hands up to help run a Friday night 'youth group'.

In the midst of all this community growth and the subsequent— and massive!—changes, Doug is the oil that encourages and enables. He offers so much of himself that it's hard for anyone to say no if he requests assistance or support.

Few ministers have Doug's extraordinary gift for pastoral care. Some will suggest that this kind of caring ought to be taken on by the church lay leaders best fitted for it. But most who are in Doug's team feel strongly that the selection of ministerial candidates is long overdue for a shift towards a Stout-style model.

1,900 years before Doug's time, another caring man wrote:

This is how we know what love is: Jesus Christ laid down his life for us. And we ought to lay down our lives for our brothers and sisters. If anyone has material possessions and sees a brother or sister in need but has no pity on them, how can the love of God be in that person? Dear children, let us not love with words or speech but with actions and in truth!

1 John 3:16-18 NIV

After departing Cromwell in late 1983, Doug Stout will live only twelve more years. He wears himself out in service to the communities which he has loved so practically and wholeheartedly, and it is little wonder that his health suffers. On Boxing Day, 1995, Doug passes away at just sixty-three years of age in Dunedin Hospital.[53]

Wherever heaven is, whatever it looks like, Doug will be there. Possibly with an adoring cat at his feet. And the kettle will be on for morning tea.

---

53 PCANZ 1996 Assembly Memorial Minute

Old Church, New Church

Benjamin Drake, the first CPC Minister

Rev Doug Stout, Minister 1976-83

Wedding party outside the old church

Isie Scott, outstanding layperson over many years

Wedding, Old Cromwell Church

Bannockburn Church, opened 1909

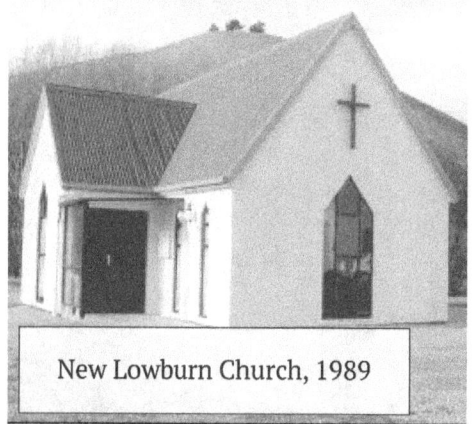

New Lowburn Church, 1989

Foster Memorial Window, Lowburn

The Caldwell family, 1993

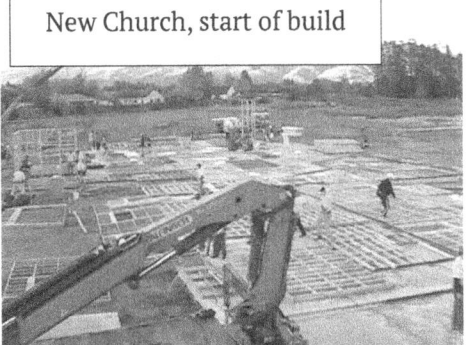

New Church, start of build

Murray Brown and Alan Wilkinson with the new church footprint

The work takes shape

Don Colling, rugby star and community leader

Fulton Hogan training at CPC

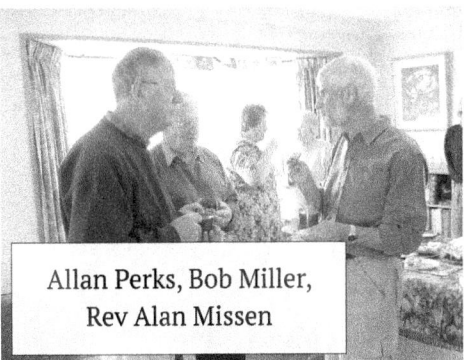

Allan Perks, Bob Miller, Rev Alan Missen

Murray and Janeice Robertson, gifted musicians

New Church opening, Myril Tutty (94) and Catherine Marshall (4)

New Church opening, Music Team

CHAPTER FIVE

Controversial and Conciliatory

IF YOU ONLY GO TO CHURCH FOR BAPTISMS, WEDDINGS and funerals, an explanation of the word 'charismatic' might help. It's a new word for most Cromwell churchgoers in the 1980s, too. If a church experiences 'charismatic renewal', there's a visible—and audible—change: Church people start talking about being 'baptised by the Holy Spirit', which means one agrees to let God completely take over your life. You talk through everything with Him by praying often—at the traffic lights, in the shower, before and after meals, at the beginning and end of meetings . . . pretty much anywhere.

Privately, you have a greater sense of God's reality, closeness and guidance; outwardly, such as in church, it often means singing livelier music, hands held above heads while singing and rocking and swaying with the rhythm. Ironically, the word fades from Christian vocabulary over time, but its impact on Christian experience since 1970 has been considerable.

Charismatic renewal has to reach Cromwell sooner or later. The town gets its first public glimpse with the so-called 'Good News 80' crusade. This takes place in the Cromwell Town Hall in 1980, with bigger crowds than Cromwell has seen for just about any event.

> *"You got just ten seconds to get on the train bound for glory . . . Don't delay, 'cos you only got five seconds now . . . Are you gonna be on this here glory train?"*

This from an African American in his thirties, snappily dressed and slick-talking. "Give me strength," whispers the man beside me. The speaker is certainly direct in his efforts to persuade the audience to become Christians. It is entertainment, almost comedy—yet we in the audience soon realise he's completely serious. At least twenty people walk up to the front to be prayed for by the speaker. While this is happening, several fall over backwards and are caught by a person stationed strategically behind them. Many in the audience are astonished. This, we learn, is called being 'slain in the Spirit'. Some locals are bemused by what they see; others are not impressed.

The charismatic movement has been around New Zealand churches, especially urban ones, for at least ten years when David Caldwell becomes minister at Cromwell in 1984. He's one of several men who have heard the call to become ministers through the leadership of the Rev John Niven at South Dunedin Presbyterian Church. David and his wife Shirley are used to trusting God completely. His way of ministering isn't strange for some CPC newcomers who have experienced similar ministry styles before coming to Cromwell—but it's *very* strange for the old guard. David is very different from their previous minister, Doug Stout, who didn't often 'lay hands' on others when praying for them (whereas David usually places his hand on the shoulder of the person being prayed for), and who didn't talk a lot about receiving the Holy Spirit.

Yes, church at Cromwell is different now. Not 'off-the-wall' different, as with *Good News 80,* but definitely different from how things used to be. People sing songs by following the words on a screen up front, rather than singing hymns from a hymn book in their hand. They often clap in time with the music or raise their hands while singing as a gesture of praise—a symbol that they want to know, or already feel God's closeness. Songs, or sections of them, are repeated two or more times. Just as with *Good News 80,* some people come up to the front to be prayed for, and there is occasionally 'laying on of hands'.

Most of the Cromwell congregation come to like this new style. It's more personal, more intimate as a way of growing faith in God. But others find it very hard going. Faith, for this second group, is supposed to be private, dignified, reflective—not shared intimately with others in a tactile, demonstrative, public way. This second group shows their faith just by being there, hearing the choir sing, saying the Lord's Prayer, singing centuries-old hymns and the Three-fold Amen at the end of a service, giving generously to the church and other good causes, and supporting church initiatives.

When the choir ceases to be a part of worship, you can almost hear the gnashing of teeth. Some of the old guard even stop coming. Helen Irwin, a church elder for fifteen years and very much loved and respected in the community, is aghast at these wholesale changes. For her, the new way verges on being phoney. She feels alienated, attends church less, gives her apology for most Session Meetings, and finally resigns in late 1986. Later, she finds some respite by going to the Anglican Church, but it's hard to drive past the Presbyterian Church on the way. She feels like something very precious has been stolen from her. Before long, she ceases to have any connection with church life at all. She is not the only elder who leaves.

Outgoing, warm and personable are all words that fit David Caldwell. He relates easily to most people. He's well enough liked in the community for the Cromwell Rugby Club to invite him to participate in an official ceremony on the occasion of their centenary in 1988. He declines when they insist their programme is fixed and advertised in advance: he'd have to be there at exactly the time of the regular Sunday service at Cromwell. Session does reach out to the Rugby Club asking them to change the time of the church parade, but they decline in turn. Is this an opportunity missed?

David Caldwell works very hard indeed within the Cromwell parish.

- He reports to Session in late 1986 that he's making a special effort at visitations before Christmas, personally visiting and getting to know members of the congregation.
- In March 1987, the church Minutes note an increased demand for David's counselling services.

- His gifts are in demand elsewhere, too; he's speaker at an Easter Camp for young people at Tirohanga, near Dunedin. He reports this as "a special time where the Spirit moved among young people attending." He's also speaker at a youth leaders' retreat in Orakanui, in February 1988.
- David's social conscience is active; he's on a local welfare committee, and he asks CPC to assist families in which the income earner has been made redundant when the Clyde Dam project winds down.
- He and Shirley, together, are in demand as leaders of several marriage enrichment weekends.
- David leads Cromwell towards becoming the sending church for new missionaries, beginning with Helen and Jim Harrington in November 1987.
- He presides over the decision to build a new church at Lowburn, with construction beginning in April 1988.
- He's involved in a spiritual renewal seminar (Wanaka), a 'Baptism of Holy Spirit' seminar (Gore), planning for a 'Life in the Spirit' seminar, a 'Life in the Spirit for Women' series, and more.

Phew! Not surprisingly, questions are asked about David's workload and priorities. Without being asked, he produces a spreadsheet analysing where his time goes, but analysis alone won't reduce his work volume. Little wonder that David Caldwell shows signs of stress and exhaustion from time to time. He needs leave to suck oxygen, regroup, reflect. There are two distinct periods in his long service to the Cromwell parish when he simply has to take a 'time out'.

David is single-minded, that we know. But he has his critics. Even people who like and usually support him, wish he wouldn't keep changing things—like moving to a single church council, dropping the choir, revising the committee system. Some also squirm with the laying on of hands in prayer: we're not all tactile and some of us need our private space.

Central amongst Caldwell's critics is a church elder who comes to Cromwell with her husband in 1979. Within three years, she's become the Session Clerk, and she holds that role for two years before the Caldwells arrive.

Over time, Caldwell begins to see this elder as an antagonist. He tells an interviewer some years later,

> *"Unfortunately, no one else was willing to stand up to her. As a consequence, Session became something of a battleground for the conflict between us."*

In 1986, the elder resigns as Cromwell's Session Clerk, in order to become clerk of the Alexandra-based Central Otago Presbytery—effectively the controlling body of Presbyterian churches throughout Central Otago at that time.

Significantly, she keeps a foothold in the Cromwell camp by remaining an elder there.

In early 1988, a proposal that the word 'Aotearoa' be inserted into the name of the national body (so as to become *Presbyterian Church of Aotearoa New Zealand* or PCANZ) provokes a strong reaction from the Cromwell Session. They vote against this change, but the local elder who is now the clerk of the Central

Otago Presbytery requests that her vote in favour of the new name be recorded in the Minutes. It is.

Then on 21 June 1988, when Cromwell elders debate a new system of committees (intended for Cromwell use only), the same elder moves:

> "... that a Session committee reflecting various views refine the proposal with reference to the Book of Order and the Central Otago Presbytery to ensure all the steps taken are in keeping with the principles and laws of the Presbyterian Church and the will of God through prayer, discussion and evaluation, and report back to the September meeting of Session, so that 1989 planning and action can be formulated."

The motion lapses for want of a seconder. Promptly, a new motion is moved:

> "... that Session approves the proposed parish structure as set out, and that Session seeks congregational approval at the forthcoming AGM."

This motion is passed and, at the AGM a few weeks later, the congregation approves.

All is not well, however; the debate has been more than robust, and signs of tension between Session members trouble the minister.

> "David Caldwell brought to the attention of Session, the question of trust between members and the concern he has for Session in this respect."

He suggests taking up Rev Ian Provan's offer to act as mediator. Session accepts, but is trust restored?

Simmering away in the background is the complicated baptism issue that will grip the Presbyterian denomination for several years. And it's personal for Caldwell: his close friend Murray Talbot has already appeared before the General Assembly in Hamilton, back in May 1988, on baptism issues. Assembly approves a committee report that recommends limited liberty of conscience in baptism issues; however, a Special General Assembly called in April 1989 suspends that decision until the May 1990 General Assembly.

Caldwell also has reservations about people who see their children's baptism as a social convention, not as a declaration of faith. Finally, in May 1989, when a couple rejects the place of faith in the baptism of their twins, he knows he can no longer conduct infant baptisms. He later confides in a friend:

> *"The moment of decision came when I conducted a baptism for twins of a Cromwell family. Despite all my efforts to instruct the parents on the significance of their child's baptism . . . it was clear they saw it simply as a cultural thing to do without any apparent faith involved. I left that day feeling that . . . the infant baptism had failed those parents and their children and successfully inoculated them from the need to make a personal response of faith."*

Caldwell writes to Session soon afterwards, seeking a special meeting in which his position can be discussed. He will no longer do infant baptisms. Immediately, things get out of hand. Caldwell explains:

"Unfortunately, the existing divisions in Session lead to some Session members contacting Presbytery before we had a chance to discuss it together. I and other members of Session feel betrayed as a result. Presbytery comes in with a heavy hand."

Two meetings are held on 23 and 30 May 1989 respectively. At the first, Caldwell supplies a list of different positions the church can take on baptism. Six out of eight Session members are loyal to David; the other two abstain. No agreement is reached at this meeting, except to bring in an outsider, Rev Iris Woods, to chair the second meeting[54]. When they do meet again, a motion is passed:

"We accept David's position provisionally and await the outcome of the May 1990 Assembly's decision on liberty of conscience."

This motion is the direct cause of Session being dissolved some three months later.

At its July meeting, Central Otago Presbytery creates a Visitation Committee. Its job is to dissuade Caldwell from refusing to baptise infants. This committee goes to Cromwell, meets with the Caldwells at 4 pm, then meets with the office-bearers at 6:15 pm. It's hard to imagine light-hearted small talk. At 8 pm, the committee meets with congregation members. Media persons are asked to leave, and once they have departed, everyone present is urged not to comment to media. Then, as the Central Otago Presbytery Minutes report, there is a 'full and open' sharing of points of view. The

---

54 The Presbyterian Church of New Zealand had been ordaining women ever since 1964. Until that time women had mainly served as deaconesses, elders, and missionaries.

committee declares itself available to meet with individuals and groups from the parish, up to 31 August. A Presbytery notice is to be read to the congregation on 13, 20 and 27 August.

At Presbytery's regular meeting (held on 10 August), Rev Dr Robyn McPhail is appointed supervisor for Rev Caldwell. This is ironic as, not very many years later, their roles will be reversed when McPhail is effectively made redundant from her post as minister at Clyde. Such 'supervision' looks like the Presbyterian hierarchy simply making sure the 'rebel' doesn't break any more rules.

Presbytery plans a meeting for 14 September in Alexandra, but things are happening quickly now, obviously due to ongoing consultations between Presbytery and the national body, PCANZ. People can't do their own thing, even if Assembly has granted 'Limited Authority'. One must toe the party line or, under Section 444 of the 'Book of Order', expect discipline.

A 'Commission of Presbytery' suddenly materialises on 11 September, three days before the Alexandra meeting. This 'Commission' involves much the same people as on the original Visitation Committee. They clearly go to Cromwell with instructions from PCANZ to sort out the problem. The showdown begins at 9:25 pm. Caldwell surrenders his licence as a Minister of the Word and the Sacraments. Central Otago Presbytery takes several actions:

(a) Says Caldwell's licence will 'lie upon the table' while Assembly makes up its mind about baptism. However, Assembly doesn't reach agreement about baptism within the two years it sets itself—instead, this process takes seven years. Caldwell only gets his licence back after the national body is prodded by Cromwell elders, who write insisting that it must happen. They wait and wait for a reply. Not a good look.

(b) Permits Caldwell to carry on as 'stated supply', effectively doing the job of the minister without being the permanent appointee, for two years. This saves them having to find another minister.

(c) Appoints new Cromwell local Bill Wilson, alongside Gerry Gillespie (of Maniototo) and Mrs Lyn Jeffery (of Queenstown), as 'Assessor Elders' to replace the Cromwell Session. Wilson, the Cromwell-based chair, must take most of the considerable flak on his own.

(d) Appoints Rev David Borne, a minister in Queenstown, as Interim Moderator.

(e) Puts a damage-control process in place. Pages 1-7 of the Report are *not* to be made public, and arrangements are made for these pages to be destroyed, including the papers of absent members.

It would be good to say that's the end of this sorry tale, but it is not.

All documents regarding this matter are put under seal in the Presbyterian Archives in Dunedin. Not to be read by anyone—not even well-meaning authors of books about the brave Cromwell Church. The ostensible reason is that the privacy of people involved might be compromised. This is very hard to explain to outsiders, who are not impressed by churches that won't—or can't—tell it like it is.

And so, dear Reader, if you've stayed valiantly through the telling of this saga, you're forgiven for thinking there must have been something to hide . . .

The following day, a press release by the Moderator of the General Assembly, Rt Rev Neil Churcher, is published in a Central Otago newspaper under the heading, "Minister's stand on baptism costs him his licence." It's a big enough story that a TV news crew hotfoots it to Cromwell. It will be many months before Cromwell has its own elders again.

David Caldwell shared a poignant recollection of these events:

> *I felt I did not have the right to take unilateral action, and I was willing to submit myself to the Church's discipline. I believe that over the period that followed, I demonstrated a willingness to do that at great cost personally, family-wise and for the congregation. If I were to have the time over again, I would simply leave.*

The clerk of the Central Otago Presbytery loses her elder status at Cromwell as part of the dismissed Session. About a year later, she seeks support from the new Cromwell Session when she applies for ministry training. It is not forthcoming, and she transfers to the Union Church at Clyde.

For the Cromwell Parish, and for the Caldwell family, the damage has been done. In June 1994, in the eleventh year of his ministry at Cromwell, David turns the other cheek in amazing fashion: he agrees to become Moderator of Central Otago

Presbytery—four years and nine months after that same body has taken his ministerial licence from him.

Just two months later, at the end of a Session meeting in August 1994, weary beyond words, he announces he'll be concluding his Cromwell ministry in January 1995. David and his family depart New Zealand to live in a Christian community in Australia. He never ministers in any church again.

Central Otago Presbytery, never slow to tighten its grip on the Cromwell parish and displaying a stunning lack of institutional self-awareness and empathy, sends a message to the Cromwell elders, asking them to "ascertain Session's view and understanding of David's resignation."

They are sent this reply:

> The Cromwell and Districts Presbyterian Church Session notes the resignation of Rev David Caldwell in January 1995 with much regret. We will be sorry to see David and Shirley leave; however, we will place no obstacle in their way and wish them every blessing as they continue following our Lord's direction.

Caldwell later writes:

> It was . . . intolerable. I was never sure if I had a position from one year to the next. My licence having been taken off me . . . my authority and legitimacy was diminished. Despite the goodwill of many in Presbytery, I felt like a leper, alienated from the Church. I recall attending Assembly . . . feeling like a problem, rather than a member. That protracted process led me to feel very disillusioned. I'd

submitted myself to the discipline of the Church but had been abused by the Church's inability to act in a pastoral manner. The costs for my family were very high. Shirley and the children paid dearly . . . it undermined the older children's respect for the Church . . .

The Caldwells' ministry remains the second longest the parish has ever had. It's clear that David played a huge part, not only as leader of the Cromwell Church but also in the collective life of Presbyterian churches in the south of New Zealand. While it's true that their charismatic ministry style alienated some, the Caldwells led many in the parish to a deeper, more active faith.

CHAPTER SIX

Missionaries Who Went

AT A TIME WHEN BEING CHRISTIAN ISN'T 'fashionable', Kiwi Christians have to be strong to go overseas as missionaries. They farewell family they may not see again; they travel vast distances to places not at all like home; they often live in sub-standard conditions, risking health, relationships and sometimes their safety. They're either insane—or their faith really matters to them.

They also have to swallow their pride, asking other people for 'support', with willing donors giving money to help cover the missionary's travel, living costs, and incidental expenses. That kind of request in one's own community takes some doing. It looks like bludging to some. Yet, for centuries, missionaries have gone cap-in-hand to ask for such help.

Most Christian mission work nowadays is based on the principle that words alone are not enough. Having faith means committing to sharing the tangible things of life:

> *Let him who has two coats give to him who has none.*
>
> *Luke 3:11*

Simple sharing, really. Christians don't have a monopoly on sharing, but for them, sharing is what you must do in a starving, hurting world . . . food, clothing, shelter. Sometimes, the very shirt off your back—not to mention time, talents and expertise such as building, engineering, and medical and teaching skills.

One of the earliest missionaries makes it clear:

> *If someone has enough money to live well and sees a brother or sister in need but shows no compassion—how can God's love be in that person? Dear children, let's not merely say that we love each other; let us show the truth by our actions.*
>
> *1 John 3:17-18 NLT*

Alan Buxton, who with his wife Edith visits the Harringtons in West Africa in the 1990s, explains:

> *There's a never-ending demand on missionary compassion. They must explain the good news in a strange tongue and different thought pattern. How can you see this through, without a personal connection in prayer to God and knowledge of the support team and prayer at home?*

Before they become overseas missionaries, Jim and Helen Harrington move to Cromwell in 1986, with Jim doing shift work on the nearby Clyde Dam. Helen is active in the community, teaching gymnastics and the piano. A short-term stint for Jim with World Vision in the Solomon Islands triggers the mission impulse, and in 1987 they go off to Bible College in Auckland. Here, Jim does cross-cultural missionary training while Helen combines part-time study and work with caring for Christine and Anita, their first two children.

By late 1989, the Harringtons are accepted by the mission agency Serving In Mission (SIM), and CPC agrees to partner with the family as their sending church. In 1990 they combine part-time work with team building and raising support. Soon, the country of Burkina Faso (an ex-French colony in Africa) and the Fulani (an unreached, nomadic, cattle-herding people) are decided upon. By year-end, the Harringtons have spoken at forty-three gatherings and have over fifty percent of their required support pledged.

1991 is a year of intensive French study, six and a half hours a day. By September, they've shared in a total of sixty-four meetings, have over five hundred recipients on their mailing list, and have their belongings packed in four 150-litre plastic drums, ready to take to Africa. Amazed at God's goodness, the family leaves New Zealand in mid-October, one hundred percent supported.

For the next eleven and a half years, the Harringtons are mostly based in Djibo—a village on the southern edge of the Sahara Desert in northern Burkina Faso, West Africa. They live on a shared compound with an extended Fulani family—a husband, two wives, two sets of children, and various relatives—as well as a menagerie of animals. Amenities are all very basic. The houses are made of mud with a cement floor, loose metal louvre windows, and a tin roof. Temperatures reach the high 40° Celsius during the hot season, so the family sleep outside all year round. Lunch meals are eaten by hand, with food shared around in common bowls; fifteen to thirty partake. They have no phone or fridge. Later, solar panels help provide a little light and power for a few small fans. One visitor describes the scene:

> *Water is too precious to wash in; much too precious for dishwashing (hens or goats lick them clean). The sick and poor surround us, constantly seeking help. Church services? There's no sense of time; people trickle in over two or three hours. Talking about God? Expect a struggle with concepts, in a language without a word to describe many ideas. Visual illustrations? Better be good. Understanding pictures is not a skill here. Sing hymns? There aren't any! You'll have to write them first.*

Every two or three months, the Harringtons travel to the capital of Ouagadougou for supplies, rest and team meetings. The two-hundred-kilometre trip takes eight hours each way. No wonder Murray Brown, a Cromwell visitor, recalls a visit to Sebba—a nine-hour round trip—causing seven flat tyres!

After dedicating their first year to learning Fulfulde (the Fulani language), Jim and Helen begin sharing their Christian faith through practical assistance: literacy, basic healthcare, the combatting of infant malnutrition, clean water and well development, transport and grain aid. Mixed throughout their hands-on service are Christian teachings offering alternative beliefs and ideals, such as: the equal value of men, women and children; being responsible for improving your own lot; assurance around eternal life. Close, lifelong friendships are made with fellow SIM team members and with many local Fulani.

The third and fourth Harrington daughters, Lydia and Phoebe, are born in Djibo with the help of good friends, Ken and Jocelyn Elliott—Australian medical missionaries who run a small, very basic hospital. When old enough, all the girls learn via the New Zealand Correspondence School. Their main teacher is their mother, but sometimes there are other helpers who stay for several months, as Alison Brown does in 1996.

Lydia's birth triggers a helpful community project. A healthy, chubby baby, she soon embarrassingly dwarfs many infants who are much older. Many of Helen's friends have small, struggling babies who are obviously short on milk. The Harringtons begin helping these babies in a more organised way, initially by making up milk (from milk powder) and supplementing feeds.

Sourcing large quantities of milk powder isn't easy. At first, the Harringtons buy twenty-kilogram sacks whenever they're down in the capital. They mix up milk and help with feeding as required. Occasionally, Helen even breast-feeds other women's babies, and a few infants spend the night in their bed. Some live, most die. Soon, mums or others caring for the malnourished babies are included in the Harrington's scope. How can you save a sick baby while watching the mum waste away? As resources allow, they help with medicine costs and small amounts of grain—enough for one week's meals.

In 1993, Haoua, a member of the extended Fulani family the Harringtons live with, begins working with them as house help and Milk Powder Project assistant. When the Harringtons return to New Zealand for furloughs in 1995 and 2000 respectively, Haoua runs the Milk Powder Project responsibly in their absence.

By the time they return to Africa for one more stint, they've bought the old Cromwell Fire Station back home. After some work, it's 'kind of liveable' when they return permanently to Cromwell in May 2003. Life after missionary postings can be trying, but God is good: both Jim and Helen have been usefully employed since they came home from Africa. Jim's building background twice provides him with roles looking after building apprentices. And Helen has been manager of the local op-shop, directing the work of more than thirty volunteers. Their life in Cromwell still sees them leading from the front, offering missionary update gatherings in their home (BYO fish and chips!), managing fundraising events like a community ball, running church camps, and running a weekly men's breakfast at 6 am on Wednesdays.

Anita is the first of the Harrington children to return to Africa when she spends five months with SIM in Burkina Faso over 2008-2009. Here's her account of this trip:

"I'm nineteen when the chance arises to join eight others in a Dunedin 'Student Soul' team going to Burkina Faso. I've wanted to return there for years! And I speak the language ... My time in Burkina is spread over four locations. First, with the Student Soul team in Ouagadougou, the capital, helping in local churches and with translating, praying for the sick and poor, helping at an orphanage.

Then I go north alone, to my home village. I spend time with a missionary family and the Fulani family I grew up with. I help with children's outreach, women's Bible studies, and the Milk Powder Project our family started. I go to isolated areas for evangelism—a huge highlight. I see my childhood through adult eyes, better appreciating my parents' sacrifice. What a privilege to be back in this special place, where I understand and fit effortlessly into the culture!

I then travel to Mahadaga, South-Western Burkina Faso, helping a lady I know well: lots of visiting, helping in a nearby clinic, more remote area visits for evangelism. I'm inspired and challenged; however, I also experience loneliness and sometimes physical fear. It's hard . . . Next, I go to Tenkodogo with the Pilkintons, a New Zealand family I know well. I look after their kids, cook and join in their work. I appreciate what this sort of help adds, having experienced it growing up in my own family.

My trip ends back in Ouagadougou. Here, I ponder returning to Africa long-term; I'm struggling with going back to New Zealand while trying to figure out how two such different worlds can co-exist. I gain clarity, peace and assurance that God will indeed have me serve long-term in missions."

Another Harrington daughter, Christine, and her husband, Pete Johnstone, are also called into overseas missions. They write:

"Things move quickly. Within six months, we're accepted by SIM. By early 2013, we sell our belongings, gather an incredible support team around us and travel to France for twelve months language study. We reach Sebba, Burkina Faso, in January 2014, and baby James arrives in June. Our time there isn't easy, always busy, but special—serving the Lord with a sense of urgency. We fall in love with Sebba, making lifelong friends there.

"But on 16 January 2016, we're woken with news of terrorist attacks in Ouagadougou killing thirty-one (including a missionary we know) and the kidnapping of our dear friends, the Elliotts, in Djibo. An armed escort is quickly organised; we have twenty minutes to pack and leave. Later, Pete makes a quick trip back for some belongings, but for the rest of us, that's goodbye. Our furlough to New Zealand is already booked for May.

"We return to Burkina Faso in January 2017, this time based at Fada N'gourma. Pete has two roles: Fulani team point person and Fada station manager. We also work with Fulani around town. Sadly, the security situation there worsens, and in May 2018 we move to Ouagadougou. Christine works three days a week in the SIM office, overseeing projects around the country; Pete meets with and encourages Fulani pastors, leaders and believers. We love getting to know students at the nearby Fulani Bible School, and Christine enjoys teaching women there.

"In December 2018, just two weeks before our scheduled return to New Zealand for baby Anna's delivery, SIM 'pauses' all Fulani-related ministries for security reasons. It's clear things will get worse; with heavy hearts, we sell our belongings and say our final goodbyes.

"Back in New Zealand, we don't know what God has next for us, but slowly, He calls us towards Niger and makes the way clear. In October 2019, we arrive in Niamey, Niger, with our children James, Abigail and Anna. We look for a vehicle and *somewhere to live, and Pete explores ministry options. Sadly, an attack close by makes us realise the terrorist threat in Burkina is spreading. Pete is now struggling with the mental, emotional and physical symptoms of PTSD. Reluctantly, we return to New Zealand in February 2020 to get help for Pete, debrief, and seek the Lord's will for whatever comes next.*

"The continuing spread of terrorism in most countries where the Fulani people live severely limits opportunities. Then COVID-19 makes travel impossible. Pete needs time and space to heal, but also work to keep him busy. We get a share-milking position near Clinton, seeing this as God's plan for our immediate future. In one sense, we're gutted and sad to be moving on from Fulani ministry; in another sense, we have peace and gratitude: God is providing this opportunity at a time when many are losing jobs."

The third Harrington daughter, Anita, and her husband, Daniel Muir, head to Botswana, Africa, in 2015. On arrival, Daniel's skills are used in information technology at Flying Mission, an SIM partner. When Flying Mission faces internal difficulties, Daniel and Anita shift focus to their neighbourhood and local church. Daniel starts men's groups and youth groups, helps with prison ministries and begins a street boys' outreach; Anita leads a women's baking and Bible study group, and a kids' outreach class. She also helps in the local Sunday School.

In 2017, SIM's partnership with Flying Mission ends. Back in New Zealand and seeking other openings with SIM, the Muirs choose Zambia. In their new home in Lusaka, they study the Lozi language. Daniel also provides IT support at SIM's office there.

When visa issues force them to leave the country, they travel down to Malawi where they celebrate their daughter Esther's fifth birthday with fellow Cromwell missionaries, Jim and Diane Young. Regrettably, on their return to Lusaka, they find many of their possessions have been stolen in a home burglary.

Six months later, the Muirs move west to Mongu near the Angolan border to work at the SIM Youth Centre. Daniel does small-group and one-on-one work, as well as maintenance and other daily tasks. Anita helps with a girls' group; she again runs a Sunday School class and some home-based outreach. There's also home-schooling to manage.

The Muirs return to New Zealand in 2018 for health reasons. When they return to Lusaka some months later, Daniel establishes discipleship programmes at local universities in partnership with the Evangelical Church of Zambia. Sadly, the health issues persist, and in September 2023, they settle permanently in New Zealand, where Daniel takes up a position as the youth pastor for St Albans Church in Palmerston North.

Jim and Helen return to Africa twice after 'coming home': over December 2017-January 2018 to visit Christine, Pete and their family in Burkina Faso; and again over August-September in 2018, to visit Anita, Daniel and their girls in Zambia. Yes, it's Mum and Dad visiting family, but it's also the veterans returning to encourage those on the front line.

The Milk Powder Project, adopted by SIM after Jim and Helen left, and supported by Cromwell Presbyterians dropping gold coins in empty two-litre milk containers every Sunday, sadly no longer functions in Djibo, although milk powder is provided in some areas where missionaries are still present. Jim and Helen have occasional contact with Haoua and Bintu, who both toiled for so long on the project in Djibo. In differing ways, the 'gold coin' idea is still pursued at Cromwell Presbyterian Church, with donations supporting children and young people in other Cromwell-linked mission projects around the world.

To everything there is a season. Well-known words from the book of Ecclesiastes in the Old Testament made famous in a song by the Byrds in 1965. Seasons don't last forever, and there's a compelling ring of urgency in the New Testament affirmation of this:

> *Work, for the night is coming when no one can work!*
>
> *John 9:4*

Wise Heads on Young Shoulders

Cromwell 1996-2001; Malawi 2003-2023

JIM AND DIANE YOUNG ARRIVE IN CROMWELL AFTER eleven years of ministry in the Wallacetown parish in Southland. That's rare for Cromwell in the 20th century—no other minister comes directly from such a long period of ministry in another church.

It's a tough assignment for the Youngs, following on from the controversial and high-profile pastorate of the Caldwells. The winding-down of the Clyde Dam workforce brings further uncertainty, but there has been substance in the work of David and Shirley Caldwell, despite the issues that have left some division within the church.

In a special Session meeting held on 7 December 1994—a few years before the Youngs arrive—interim pastor Helen Dick explains that the focus of her call as Stated Supply Minister to Cromwell will be 'conflict resolution'. She knows David's ministry has been good for the parish, but there are some old issues floating around which still need settling.

For example, the parents of a child baptised in April 1995 aren't willing to be involved in the worship service and so attend only the baptism part. Some communicants don't mind; as they see it, at least the parents came, and their child is baptised in the church. It's better to have this connection with an 'outside' family than no connection at all. Compromise? Through the eyes of a few, perhaps . . .

Finding elders is another problem—one that is all too familiar in most country parishes, not just in Cromwell. When the Session was summarily dismissed by the Central Otago Presbytery in 1989, there were two husband-and-wife teams on Session. Six years later, in July 1995, there are two Hansens, and two Robertsons in a Session that still only has seven members. The individuals concerned have been terrific contributors to CPC life over many years, but there's still a sense that leadership should ideally be spread over a wider range of people. It's really a matter of who will put their hands up to do the work. But after the Caldwell saga, you can't blame people for avoiding a task from which the centralised authorities might dismiss you if they don't like what you do . . .

At the 1995 AGM, held in August, the seriousness of CPC's financial situation is raised. Presbytery will give permission to call another minister, but only if another $10,000 is added to the projected income. Somehow, that money must have been found, as the Session Minutes of 12 March 1996 record the passing of a motion "that the Rev James Young be invited to be the next minister of this parish." This is confirmed at a congregational meeting on 17 March, and the Youngs are inducted in August 1996.

CHURCHES OF THE LATE 20TH AND EARLY 21ST CENTURIES operate in a vastly different world from that of fifty years earlier. New issues are surfacing, reflecting the more secular and liberal society emerging in New Zealand. For example, the outgoing correspondence of 12 December 1995 records that the Cromwell Church wished to disassociate itself from a PCANZ decision to approve a practising homosexual graduate in theology for service as a minister.

However, within a year of Jim Young becoming minister, Cromwell does endorse a 1996 General Assembly motion allowing some latitude for homosexual leaders, "so long as compassion does not overshadow biblical truths." But this issue doesn't go away. A study group led by Clif Tapper reports much division within the group. Murray Brown, CPC delegate to the 1998 General Assembly, shares a similar story: 54% were against, 46% were for, in a vote on homosexuals being engaged in Presbyterian church leadership.

Sexuality matters were, and are, a minefield for Presbyterians, as well as for New Zealand society as a whole. The Minutes of a special meeting on 19 August 1997 note that, "Two couples who are members of the congregation are living together though not married, despite previous admonitions from Session."

Previous admonitions? Is Session telling its people what they can and can't do?

Echoes of the *kirk* (a Scottish word for church) hauling the poet Robbie Burns and his lover Jeanie up for a public scolding in church come to mind. The church's authority to discipline would probably have gone unchallenged a generation or so earlier, but not now. There's a complaint from one of the couples who have been 'admonished'. Alan Paulin, a widely respected layman and the headmaster-emeritus of John McGlashan College, is sent by Presbyterian authorities to investigate. Many voice their opinions, and Mr Paulin recommends that "Session could perhaps lean more towards grace in future situations." Cromwell Presbyterian Church is yet again under fire, however gently it is being phrased.

A few months later, Jim Young writes, "A pastor needs to balance between loving the people and challenging them." It's hard to argue with that. Jim's a humble fellow, but he's never been afraid to defend the biblical view when he thinks it's being ignored. He writes to PCANZ's Commission on Diversity to do exactly that, pointing out what the Bible says about homosexuality.

AT THE AGM ON 19 AUGUST 1997, LONG-TIME ORGANIST Alison Smith asks that a mention be made in the Annual Report regarding Diane Young's fine work with mothers and young children. Diane has put her medical practitioner career on hold while she has children herself. She also co-ordinates a lunchtime study group, and she runs an early equivalent of Mainly Music for young children and their mums. Grass has no chance of growing under the feet of Diane Young. Later, the Youngs admit their sadness over how few 'graduate' from the very popular Mainly Music into the church itself.

The matter of the church buildings is now becoming urgent—and increasingly public. Ross Hansen asks if we're going to keep pouring money into the rusty parish car. Alan Buxton recalls both the poor condition of the roof and the extreme difficulty in accessing it for repair purposes.

The possible purchase of a building in the local mall is mooted in August 1997, and with that suggestion, the future of all three existing sites (Bannockburn, Cromwell, and Lowburn) is called into focus. Not surprisingly, the Bannockburn community wants to keep their building. A year later in August 2000, Rev Pete Willsman from East Taieri chairs the first comprehensive look at the building issues. There's much verbal to-ing and fro-ing, but a consensus is eventually reached: a new building will be required.

Jim, however, won't be presiding over the journey towards a new church building. In July 2000, he informs Session that he is torn between attending a missionary outreach course in Matamata—his preference—and going to Assembly. The Minutes of 3 August 2000 record Jim taking study leave for three weeks. He and Diane go to the Matamata event to discern "whether this is a way for their future." In October, Jim shares that he and Diane "are seriously looking ahead." The call to overseas mission is strong for them, and Diane is eager to get back into medicine again. On 9 November 2000, Jim indicates that 30 June 2001 is the date he will cease to be CPC's parish minister. A fortnight after this, on 15 July 2001, a service of celebration is held for the Youngs, following four years and ten months of service. No minister has striven more faithfully; and no minister's wife has contributed more to parish life than Diane—who, just one month later, is successfully re-registered to practice medicine.

Life has certainly not been dull under Jim and Diane's watch. Highlights include the Bannockburn Faith Festival, orchestrated by Christine Hansen in 1997; Christmas nativity plays, such as *A Good Night's Sleep* in 1999; Easter choirs energetically led by Joan Hunter; raising money for radio equipment to ensure reception of the Christian radio stations Rhema, Star and Life FM in Cromwell. A 'March for Jesus' in early 1999 is a forerunner of the Good Friday interdenominational marches which are still going twenty-five years later. There are also progressive dinners which are good for bonding CPC people in fellowship and hospitality.

There's a note of wistfulness in Jim's voice today when he reminisces about his years as a minister in Cromwell. He's sad that, while the Word has been preached faithfully, much of it has fallen—in terms of the Parable of the Sower—on stony ground. Humble to the last, he's almost certainly a bit hard on himself regarding this . . .

In typically self-effacing style, Jim looks after the children while Diane works in general practice in Alexandra. Diane then goes off to do a tropical medicine course in Glasgow, Scotland. In early 2003, the Young family arrives in Malawi where they will serve for fifteen years.

Back when they first agreed to lead the Cromwell parish, Jim and Diane knew that overseas missions would be God's persistent beckoning to them. They have long been mindful of the importance of Sunday School work—an area which later becomes a focus of their mission work in Malawi—and Jim and several others recall more than one Sunday when he walked out of a church service he was leading because "there was no one to take the Sunday School." It wasn't a stunt—it was Jim recognising the need to reach children first if the church is to grow. There was never a tirade aimed at the congregation or a raised voice on Jim's part. He simply explained the need in a couple of simple sentences, then went off to run the Sunday School class.

This struggle for Sunday School facilitators is a graphic echo of something Jesus says:

> *"The fields are ready for harvest, but there are few willing to do the work!"*
>
> *Matthew 9:37*

Mission support from the Cromwell parish is strong for the Youngs, as it has been for other long-term Cromwell missionaries—the Harringtons in Africa and the Potters in Thailand. Their integrity is beyond question, but few understand how much preparation is needed for people from first-world, wealthy countries to transition as missionaries to very poor countries. Nor do they understand how agonising such choices can be in terms of their personal lives, their families, their future. For example, boarding school life doesn't suit every child at every stage in their lives. And many missionaries can testify to that.

During May-June of 2012, Marie Stiven and Edith Geddis make a 'life-changing' trip to visit the Youngs in Malawi. Marie reports:

> *"We went with Jim to remote locations where he'd arranged day-long teaching sessions for Sunday School teachers. We each delivered three seminars on aspects of children's work, repeating these at each location. We also spent time with Diane in the hospital and epilepsy clinics.*

Jim and Diane show us what commitment and selflessness mean in mostly very challenging circumstances. They clearly bond with the people, trying to show God's love in every way possible.

One lasting memory involves a mother who carried her disabled child for four or five hours to get treatment at the epilepsy clinic. She must have repeated the journey home that same day, in the dark, through the bush. It has since been possible to buy bicycles for such needs, but to this day, whenever I'm feeling sorry for myself, I think of that mother and ask for forgiveness."

Six years later, over June-July 2018, Marie Stiven returns with Barbara Carston, timing their visit just before the end of the Young's service in Malawi. Edith Buxton, another Cromwell member, is meant to be part of this trip also, but unfortunately, serious illness prevents her from joining them. Again, Marie shares her observations:

"Barbara and I join others from East Taieri Church to visit Jim and Diane Young, who are working with SIM, partnering with the local African Evangelical Church in Malawi.

We go to support the Youngs. Jim asks if we can fundraise to buy iron for three churches' roofs. After serious fundraising, $27,000 is found for this purpose. We also go to contribute to the churches Jim is involved with, working mainly in the three churches mentioned above—taking ladies' meetings, teaching and sharing handcraft skills. The men meet separately. We gather in half-finished brick buildings, reed-covered *stick shelters, a hired marquee and a fully finished church. Everywhere we go, we meet dedicated ministers and smiling, friendly people—and on all sides, we encounter deep poverty.*

We spend a day in a village doing malaria testing, and two days working with Diane in the Epilepsy Clinic she's established. There, I'm privileged to pray with each client. We meet Jim's STUM (Sunday School Teachers United Movement) training team, and we're guests at Jim and Diane's farewell. They're soon to return to New Zealand, and we hear endless grateful tributes to them at the national church's Sunday farewell—a six-hour service!

Do we help people during this visit? I'm not sure. I hope our visit reminds them they're not alone or forgotten, and that New Zealand Christians think of and pray for them—just as they pray for us. I do know the impression that they who have so little make on me. I'm humbled, challenged, awestruck and thankful."

In 2018, after fifteen years of fine work sharing the Christian faith and giving medical attention to the people of Malawi, the Youngs return to New Zealand. They settle in Ashburton, an hour south of Christchurch in the South Island. At a time when GPs are in desperately short supply, Diane soon finds herself working shifts at a local practice. In all their endeavours, she and Jim typify a 'giving' view of life, as much as anyone this author has ever known.

CHAPTER EIGHT

From the Old to the New: We Did It in Two!

MORE THAN ONE HUNDRED YEARS WILL PASS after the fine new church's 1881 opening before any Presbyterian in Cromwell gives serious thought to the idea that the building may not be fit for purpose much longer. The simple truth is that there are a lot more people in town now. The influx of workers associated either directly or indirectly with the building of the new Clyde Dam has been huge, and while the old church was built on the south-east perimeter of town— just right for the Cromwell of the late 19th century—the 21st-century town will have a new centre of activity almost two kilometres away to the west and north. Add to that the maintenance issues that are occurring more and more often with the old building, and the case for contemplating a change is clear enough.

There are plenty of strong opinions. The first task is to separate outsiders with strong opinions from actual practising attendees of the Presbyterian Church. Some of these 'outsiders' are really lapsed 'insiders'—people who were active in the church but haven't been involved for a long time. This means making sure that the church roll of 'communicant Presbyterians' is up to date. Once that's done, the next challenge is getting these 'communicants' to decide whether to sell the existing church and build a new one or to stay put and repair and extend the one-hundred-year-old building.

You can't blame those in favour of a new building for calling meetings where interested members/adherents must be present to hear the debate. The opponents of rebuilding are bound to think the Building Committee is going too fast and not being considerate of people with alternative ideas which could mean keeping the old church. Equally, the Building Committee grows impatient with the stone-walling tactics of those who simply don't want to shift at all.

Anthony Young, a local Justice of the Peace, has retired in Cromwell with his wife, Carol. Before coming to Cromwell, the Youngs led a massive effort to build a hall and community centre in Mossburn, Southland, where they farmed for many years. Anthony feels sure that, with modern engineering, the old church building can be upgraded and extended to provide the extra facilities it will need for a growing congregation. His is the most constructive attempt to offer an alternative to rebuilding from the ground up.

Then follows a debate on many levels:

- The traditional building (currently on a great site above the point at which the two rivers meet) vs. the new building (suggested to be placed on a site in the town's new business area, making it more central than the old site).
- For long-standing members, old buildings equate to a very traditional faith and a corresponding view about how worship should be. There was—and is—a sense of following in the footsteps of previous generations: same faith, same building.
- The perceived worth of the views of longer-standing Cromwell residents vs. the views of newer arrivals. It would be nice if old and new could accept each other from day one, but it is not always so.
- A traditional view of God—definite views, not often spoken out loud—vs. an evangelical outlook: If you have faith and it's worth having, then you should be sharing it with other people.

If you've been wondering why this church's official title is 'Cromwell and Districts Presbyterian Church', this part of the parish journey illustrates it well. Little communities like Bannockburn and Lowburn are fiercely parochial. They've always had their own clubs and activities, and they continue to do so. Bannockburn's Bowls Club is respected far and wide, and the ice rink in Lowburn is the seat of curling around here. The gold rush brought many people to live in Bannockburn; even if they aren't all churchgoers, they grew up in an age of respecting churches and expecting there to be one where they live.

When the Presbyterian Church first arrived in gold-rush Central Otago, parishes often covered three or more small towns, as well as the one they were based in. Ministers were expected to take services on any given Sunday in at least one of the smaller towns, as well as the base church. Cromwell has, at different times in its history, run services in Bannockburn, Kawarau Gorge, Ripponvale, Lowburn and Bendigo. In addition, between 1940 and 1986, the Cromwell minister could be running services for at least one of either Arrowtown, Crown Terrace, Speargrass Flat or Gibbston.

When the Bannockburn population reached its height in the 1870s, it was a no-brainer for church and local community leaders to plan a church building there. This venture took another thirty years, but it was completed and opened in 1909. And get this: the church was built mainly by Bannockburn voluntary labour, whether or not they were church people. Regrettably, shrinkage in local population numbers and church attendance meant that services in this building ceased in the 1980s, except for funerals, weddings and an annual interdenominational carol service held before Christmas.

Fast-forward to 2002. An article appears in the Otago Daily Times of 13 June, page 13, with the heading: 'Sale of three churches may fund new building'. There's outrage in Bannockburn. "We built it! It's not yours to sell!" is the cry. Technically, empowered by Acts of Parliament, the Bannockburn building is indeed owned by the Presbyterian Church, but it's not hard to see why there is angst among Bannockburnians.

Eventually, to the surprise of many and the delight of the Bannockburn folk—whose fundraising to buy 'their' church has not been wildly successful—the Central Otago District Council steps up to the unaccustomed role of peacemaker and saves the day by buying the church as a community asset.

For CPC, there are more high hurdles to get over, including a couple of false starts regarding the site for the new church—they buy and sell sites behind the Police Station in the 1990s, and spend a lot of time considering the Post Office site before deciding it doesn't have enough room. The main obstacle now, however, is getting the congregation to vote 'Yes' emphatically enough that the Central Otago Presbytery will decide it's a good idea and give the required assent.

However, 'assent' from Presbytery is certainly not the same thing as funding. Funding is duly sought from the 'parent church', but when push comes to shove, Cromwell receives encouraging words from the Presbyterian hierarchy, lots of quasi-political control, but less than 10% of the actual cost.

You have to love the next part of the story. After various polls to measure churchgoers' enthusiasm for the latest plan, there's still hesitation, even over plans to build on the more promising site in Elspeth Street where, incidentally, the church stands today in 2024. Murray Brown, who has stoically borne the burden of leading this project for almost twenty years, is persuaded by Alan Wilkinson to create what you might call a 'eureka moment'. One Sunday evening in 2004, the congregation has stayed in the church, not making much progress in yet another meeting, mainly because the latest cost estimate is much higher than expected. Suddenly, a ram's horn sounds from the balcony above and behind them. Wilkinson and Brown march down the stairs, and Wilkinson declares: "It's time! I have the answer!"

The stunned parishioners then hear the plan that will make news all around New Zealand, saving the church almost a million dollars on building costs. Wilkinson declares he can use his influence to source tradies willing to give their time and expertise (and, in many cases, materials) over two days; this will lead to the roof being on and the building being at 'close-in' stage, with CPC people finishing the interior themselves. Alan Buxton leaps to his feet and says, "Let's do it!" The meeting agrees, the long battle is over, and the 'We Did It in Two' project is born.

Alan Wilkinson is as good as his word. Three building firms put their hands up when approached by him: Don Colling Construction, Wedge Construction and O'Callaghan and Walker. Looking back, Don Colling says he just knew the project would be good for Cromwell, as well as a good way to give back to the town. His contribution to the life of the town has been lifelong; apart from his prowess as an Otago rugby player and captain, he has been a Cromwell College Board member and is, at the time of writing, still active in the MenzShed group that gives voluntary practical help to householders around town. Don is a former publican of the Middle Pub. His leadership of the 'We Did It in Two' project is a reminder to church folk and pub patrons alike of the need to be careful not to judge those who are not like us. Other tradies in town soon realise this is the kind of community effort you just have to be part of, and they take up the cause too.

The project takes place in March 2006 and is meticulously organised: coloured T-shirts identify the different building teams; Wilkinson buzzes around like a hyperactive bumble bee, keeping the show on the road; former professional caterer Edith McKay ensures the workers are well fed, and food is generously donated by a wide range of people. It's heartening to have practical support from both the community in general and the other Cromwell churches. No one minds when adverse weather pushes the job into a third day. Besides, the media have turned up in droves! Good news is too good to miss. As 2006 progresses, the interior work is gradually completed by church volunteers. Fifteen months after 'We Did It in Two', the new church is officially opened in late June 2007.

The opening is a big event. And in true Cromwell style, not without incident. Edith McKay, the professional cook, is in hospital with a broken leg, and so gives instruction to Christine Hansen, the extremely able amateur cook who has never used the new kitchen before now. Alan Wilkinson can't come because of the snow which arrives all over the South Island and also strands the National Moderator of the Presbyterian Church, The Right Rev Pamela Tankersley, and prevents her from being on-site when she declares the building open by phone from Christchurch Airport. It's never simple in Cromwell, but we go on.

Alan Missen, CPC's minister since 2003, has been the right leader to simultaneously keep the project rolling and church life ticking over. But he's acutely aware of the stresses that have occurred along the way. During 2006, external facilitators run a church appraisal; in February 2007, one month before the opening of the new buildings, a report is filed with Central Otago Presbytery. An excerpt from that report reads as follows:

WE SEE OURSELVES AS A TRANSITIONING PEOPLE

1. Transitioning has been a town and community factor for the past thirty years. Major growth, new people, burgeoning industry and changes brought about by the Clyde Dam project changed Cromwell from a slow-moving Central Otago holiday spot where everyone knew their neighbour, into a less personal place to live.

2. With population growth of around 30% in the past five years, the community has changed. People are changing. Cromwell has become a service town. Future rapid change is inevitable.

3. Social changes have affected the church: a sense of not keeping up with change, of feeling like a minority, many new people coming into the church, trying to grapple with the future but looking back to the past—all this is very challenging and raises some inner disquiet amongst many.

4. Transitioning through acceptance of worship styles has been and is a major factor. The parish worshipped in two separate places with distinctly separate styles of worship. There's been a stand-off over contemporary versus traditional styles, but now there's the beginning of . . . differences and styles becoming accepted and affirmed. Alan's teaching and Session's leadership are positive influences in this area.

5. A major transition has involved a protracted and at times very painful journey of selling the old Cromwell and Bannockburn churches and the Cromwell manse, through to a united commitment to build the new complex. We experienced

considerable pain in letting go. With good leadership, vision and determination, we've seen the project through to the present excitement about officially opening and fully utilising the church complex ... a course has been steered through the building process without splitting the church ... A positive spin-off has been many people seeing 'grey heads' and the 'younger brigade' teamed up together in the manual building work.

6. Like many churches, Cromwell has transitioned to a more multi-denominational, modern church. While our Presbyterian heritage and authority is recognised, many of us ... see ourselves as cross-denominational. Many of us are torn between holding onto Presbyterian traditions and attempting to be relevant by doing church in a new way.

7. Amid changes in the town and society, we recognise differences, work at acceptance, and admit to the necessity to forgive and move on where hurt has prevailed. We recognise that nagging criticism and contention shared in any public way by comment or innuendo will negate true fellowship. We need to major on and celebrate the joy of differences.

8. Our leaders are open to the positive new opportunity that the new church complex offers, as we develop a stronger collective image of being God's people who try to care for each other in ... unselfish ways.

There are stumblings, too, as the new complex gets put into use. The use of alcohol is a contentious issue—some Christians drink, some don't. The early policy is that alcohol may be consumed in modest amounts. A rugby club event with a prominent All Black as speaker brings so much alcohol that drunkenness and vomiting are a problem, both for those on-site that night and for those cleaning up later. With the clearer light of retrospect, that event may have made life simpler for the church: the consequence of the night's excessive drinking is that a 'no alcohol' rule is put in place. And though there are a few mutterings by subsequent users of the complex, it has stayed that way ever since.

There are three claims to ownership of the new church, in no particular order. All three have a case, and, it can be argued, all parties tend towards a blinkered view.

> **1. Jointly owned by the community and the local church**: the community provides the vast majority of materials, labour and expertise; the church arranges the design work and most of the funds.

> **2. Owned solely by the local church**, because it's primarily a church and a place of worship: the church are main users, site managers, and allocators of space for both church and outside users.

> **3. Owned by, and answerable to, the Presbyterian Presbytery/Synod power hierarchy:** all Presbyterian church property in Otago is owned by the Otago Foundation Trust. If, in the fullness of time, the property is sold, that Trust determines what happens to the Funds.

There are elements of truth in all three views, and we should be glad there has been a partnership at all, however disappointed the partners may have been with each other at times.

Alan Missen's ministry ends eighteen months after the new church is opened when he accepts a call to the Rangiora Presbyterian Church. He's a fine preacher, an incisive thinker, and a capable chairperson, and in 2022 he does excellent work leading a review of the Southern Presbytery's work. Alan has been particularly appreciated by the older members of the congregation. Sixteen years after his ministry in Cromwell ends, he still visits former elders, Allan and Sandra Perks, and takes them communion.

It hasn't always been plain sailing for the Missen family in Cromwell, but Alan has done a sterling job of guiding the church in the years leading up to the 'We Did It in Two' quick build, presiding over a congregation struggling to accept both the need for change and the shape such change might take. Alan has borne a considerable burden during this time, as has Murray Brown, the project co-ordinator.

Later, Alan is on the receiving end of conflict with a church office receptionist, who seems to believe his reception role should include speaking for the minister and for the church as and when he sees fit. Another minor issue faced by the Missens is that Alan's wife, Sue, a fine musician, does not fit the traditional mould of the minister's wife, as background support for the minister; furthermore, her professional life as a counsellor is sometimes misunderstood in the parish. Sadly, Sue passes away in 2023. Still, Alan remains a regular visitor to Cromwell and retains a deep affection for the church here. His has been a significant contribution indeed.

Church people are just human, like everyone else. They lose their cool. They say hard things and later wish they hadn't. Sometimes, they fail to do the 'putting right' actions that, deep down, they know they should do. *So why is being a Christian worth it?* Because God can still use them to make the lives of people around them more liveable. When Christians allow Him to give them strength to do that, they're happier—and so are the people on the receiving end.

CHAPTER NINE

Unexpected Change

ROB PENDREIGH IS A TRUE 'MAN'S MAN', A RARE find in an era where many ministers don't fit that mould. He even invites men to his house to watch rugby tests together! Rob has life and personality and a sense of humour. He's always willing to roll up his sleeves and attack a task, as is evident when, on three separate occasions, he goes to Northern Thailand to assist with the work being done there by Cromwell missionaries Malcolm and Sandy Potter. Rob's beginnings of ministry in the far north of New Zealand have been difficult—there has even been a home invasion—so his shift to the deep south with his wife, Erin, seems very much like the right move for them.

There is so much to celebrate, especially in the first three years or so of Rob's ministry. His annual report, written for the AGM in August 2013, is full of energy and optimism. He is effusive about Catherine Forsyth's 'commitment and dedication' to her new role as leader of family ministries, noting that, "She shines the light of Christ upon individuals and families alike." Rob is also obviously delighted about *Carols on the Greenway* and *The Easter Walk of the Cross* which saw numbers involved and "were directed predominantly by CPC members." The church has been thriving, it seems, so much so that long-serving Session Clerk Christine Hansen resigns, at Rob's suggestion. She stays on Session, continuing a staggering record of service in virtually every leadership role the church has. She is replaced as clerk by Wayne Bell, but for personal reasons, his service is relatively short, and he is in turn replaced by Kathy Birtles.

Kathy does her best to support the new minister and his wife, and she becomes a close friend of Erin's. What's not initially evident to the people of Cromwell is that Erin aspires to become a minister herself. That's not unreasonable; she completes her theology degree in 2012.

Things start getting difficult when Erin wants to train under Rob's supervision. Awkward conversations take place. It's agreed that she'd be better working in the Wakatipu and Arrowtown parishes, with more objective supervision from Reverend Ian Guy and Dr Deborah Bower.

Although Rob has spoken in glowing terms about Catherine Forsyth's work as Children and Family's Worker in the 2013 Annual Report, regrettably, tensions emerge before long. Catherine is by no means a whinger, but finding herself in an increasingly hostile climate, she finds her role untenable and resigns. Eyebrows are raised in Cromwell circles, as they would be anywhere.

Meanwhile, Erin's training for ministry, Queenstown-based, is advancing. Session receives a proposal from the Pendreighs for a husband-and-wife ministry team. There is division within Session over this, for three reasons:

First, the parish would face an extra financial burden, and there is no money for this;

Second, normal selection processes would apparently be bypassed; and

Third—and perhaps most significantly—the Pendreighs seem to feel this has long been their expectation, perhaps even their entitlement, based on discussions with Cromwell leadership. However, their intention isn't in writing and comes as news to most Session members.

Two Session members resign, affected at least in part by the tension this matter is generating. Kathy Birtles, the Session Clerk, and the Pendreighs themselves, contact Presbytery. By late 2014, Alan Judge, the executive officer of the relatively new Southern Presbytery (covering all Otago and Southland Presbyterian churches) writes formally to Cromwell Session to indicate that a Commission is being appointed to come to Cromwell and sort this matter out.

Unfortunately, two members of this three-person Commission are the Reverend Ian Guy and Dr Deborah Bower—both respected and able people, but as previously indicated, both have been supervisors of Erin Pendreigh's on-the-job training. Arms-length independence is vital in such sensitive situations, but it isn't to be found here. Even more unfortunately, the findings of this Presbytery Commission are not made available to Cromwell Session members. In the years since then, there will be a lingering disappointment with Presbytery at CPC, verging on mistrust.

Kathy Birtles resigns from all her Cromwell Presbyterian connections, very displeased with the church's rejection of the joint ministry proposal. She has given strong leadership within the church for more than fifteen years and will be missed.

Rob Pendreigh has a painful attack of myalgia which affects his heart. There's no doubt he's become increasingly stressed, whatever the causes. In 2015, Rob resigns. Presbytery directs Cromwell to pay him for study leave he hasn't taken up and also for annual leave due to him. This payment does at least mean the Pendreighs have income which takes them to early March 2016, when Rob starts as minister at Balclutha Presbyterian Church.

The Balclutha position is 0.75% of the full stipend initially (arguably, below the minimum wage equivalent), but one year later, Rob becomes full-time in the role and has been happily in ministry there for the past eight years, relaxed and in excellent health. He retains warm feelings for the Cromwell Presbyterians, and that feeling is reciprocated.

In May 2015, before their shift to Balclutha, Erin takes up a new role, working for Synod as 'Mission Advisor' to churches in Otago and Southland. Her eloquence and forthrightness fit her well for her appointment the following year as the Presbyterian Women's delegate to a United Nations Commission on the Status of Women Conference to be held in New York. Soon afterwards, in June 2016, Erin steps into another national role as Transitional Co-ordinator for 'Presbyterian Women Aotearoa New Zealand'. Other similar roles have followed since then.

It will be two long years before Cromwell has another minister. Again, that's not a decision for CPC leadership until a green light is given by Presbytery officials, and they aren't ready to do that, it seems. First, they send the very experienced former lawyer Rev Dr Kerry Enright to Cromwell as Interim Moderator. That's a big call because he is the full-time minister of Knox Presbyterian Church in Dunedin. How will he run two churches at once?

Enright is reputed to be at the liberal end of the spectrum of Presbyterian ministers, which is not the Cromwell way. Amazingly, the outcome is better than anyone in Cromwell expects—before long, he recommends to Presbytery that Cromwell be allowed to appoint a new minister. Kerry too admits to having been surprised and pleased by what he found at CPC. He laughingly comments that some of his critics at Knox thought he was at the *other* end of the spectrum, and too evangelical!

New elder Mervyn Mitchell is appointed Session Clerk at his first meeting, at which there are three other new elders present. He's been over ten years as Session Clerk in Clinton, so he's used to the Presbyterian way of doing things. He admits he expected difficulties relating to Enright. But they get on very well, often communicating by early morning and late evening phone calls, which wouldn't have worked if there'd been any tension between them.

Mitchell shows a real will to get things right as the new leader of this Session. A local brother and sister, middle–aged, throw CPC leaders into some confusion when they park their car behind the church building and sleep on the back seat for several nights. A family business has collapsed, and things have gone downhill from there. Mervyn Mitchell doggedly pursues local welfare authorities to help set up viable living arrangements which naturally don't include sleeping in their car at the church.

Unhappily, Session now asserts itself in other matters in a rather more controversial style, even with Interim Moderator Enright in the driving seat. The CPC communicant widow of a man with Masonic Lodge connections is effectively forced to hastily shift her husband's funeral to a local hotel conference room. Outrage at this is made worse because initially, CPC agrees to host the funeral, and a notice appears in the Otago Daily Times; the invitation is subsequently withdrawn when the family ask for a Masonic leader to be allowed to offer a brief farewell ritual in the funeral. In a separate matter, a young Moslem businessman is turned away when he asks if he can hold his one-year-old child's birthday party in the foyer at CPC.

There's tension within the church and within Session itself over both these matters. One Session member, Christine Hansen, approaches the grieving family of the Masonic Lodge man to try and smooth the troubled waters; another, Trevor McKinlay, plays a portable organ at the funeral held in the hotel and subsequently resigns from Session; a third Session member, Stewart Bolger, attends and is made very welcome at the Moslem child's birthday celebration, obviously at another location.

The question persists for all at CPC: How inclusive should we as Christians be? Masonic rites in some parts of the world are said, at their extreme, to be dark—even demonic—and are not surprisingly spurned by Christians. But CPC's decision to turn away the widow of the Cromwell man—and the Moslem man wanting a birthday party for his son—are rejected in Cromwell both within and outside the church. Are these refusals acts of love, even if they represent Christian leaders just trying to be true to their consciences and stand firm against ideas and beliefs they firmly believe are wrong, even evil?

Dear Reader, please bear with the author, who finds two truths to consider in this:

> 1. We who try to follow the Christian pathway will keep doing dumb things, just like other normal humans in the secular world, including getting upset with each other;

> 2. We are nevertheless forgiven, renewed, and strengthened by the grace of God, to pick ourselves up and start again, day by day.

Perhaps it's best explained in the words of the New Testament:

For now we see as if looking through darkened glass; one day, we'll see Jesus, face to face. For now, we have three special gifts from God: faith, hope and love. And the greatest of these is love.
                                                    I Corinthians 13:12-13

Interim Moderator, Kerry Enright, can't keep running two churches situated 230 kilometres apart, and soon another experienced minister, Alastair Smales, comes to Cromwell to continue the interim ministry, along with his wife, Jacquie. Yes—more fill-in, relieving, 'stated supply' for CPC. Still, Alastair is diplomatic, warm, and much appreciated during his eight months in this role. The good news is that both Kerry and Alastair soon believe CPC is ready for another minister. They report positively to Presbytery along these lines, probably surprising their listeners with their optimism for CPC's future.

So it is that, in March 2018, after yet another extensive search, Reverend Douglas Bradley is welcomed to Cromwell, along with his wife, Judy. The dignitaries of the Southern Presbytery and Synod are well represented. There is formal ceremony, laughter, and an excellent shared supper. By now, Cromwell Presbyterian Church has been running for 143 years, with no plans to quit.

CHAPTER TEN

More Change from Left Field

AFTER THE LONG VACANCY SINCE ROB PENDREIGH'S resignation in December 2015—two years and four months—Douglas Bradley is commissioned in March 2018. It is a happy event: other Central Otago Presbyterians and dignitaries representing the wider Otago-Southland region are present in numbers.

The reserve southerners are alleged to have towards Aucklanders is not in evidence. The Bradleys' arrival in Cromwell is a matter of some joy, even excitement.

Douglas was, and is, a North Islander. More than that, he's used to city life, and his professional experience first as a secondary school physics teacher and later, as a minister, has been in city environments in Auckland before he came to Cromwell. His wife, Judy, is an extremely competent nurse, and during their time in

Cromwell, she is often called upon by Dunstan Hospital, twenty-three kilometres away in Clyde.

Douglas is yet another Cromwell minister who believes the Christian gospel is for sharing around the world. It's recorded in the Bible as one of the last things Jesus says to His disciples:

> *"Go into the whole world and preach the gospel."*
> *Matthew 11:28 NASB*

Down through the centuries, there have been many challenges to the authority of the Bible, but for most Christians today, it's still seen as 'God's Word', and there are plenty of reputable translations available. (Even if you're one of those who struggles with the claim that the Bible is God's Word, there's still plenty of good advice in there to take notice of!)

In September-October 2019, just eighteen months into his time in Cromwell, Douglas and his good friend Ben Dykman, minister at Greenlane Presbyterian Church, accept an invitation from church leaders in rural India and travel there to lead seminars at a conference of pastors. The conference is at a training centre in the foothills of a region that has many isolated tribal villages. About fifty pastors travel up to two hundred kilometres for the week-long conference. Between them, Douglas and Ben teach seven to eight hours a day using translators. Ben teaches verse by verse through the New Testament book of Ephesians while Douglas teaches on finding Christ in the Joseph story (Genesis 37-50).

VERY FEW COULD HAVE SEEN THE COVID PANDEMIC coming, and even fewer could have seen what effect such an affliction would have on the church. Sadly, during the COVID outbreak, Douglas Bradley is subjected to sharp-tongued criticism which has only one tiny semblance of merit—it's spoken to his face. But it's unwarranted! To his great credit, Douglas carries out the scriptural exhortation to the letter: *"If any man asks you to go a mile with him, go two miles with him!" (Matthew 5:41).*

Bradley does not openly remonstrate with his critics, nor does he just throw his hands in the air and declare it all to be too hard. Outside of lockdown, Cromwell achieves something few churches of any denomination manage around the country: it runs a service for the anti-vaxxers as well as another simultaneously for those doing what the government requires of them. Awkward? Yes, but it's done. During lockdown, Bradley sharpens up his IT skills and arranges for services to be online. They are delivered on time, in a very acceptable format, as if this were something churches do every day.

That said, the cost to Bradley in stress is high. He and Judy have had family crises of one sort or another throughout their time in the South Island and have often gone north at shortish notice to deal with these. Regrettably, the personal attacks during COVID are not only less than Christian in nature; they are also unlikely to prolong the Bradleys' ministry in Cromwell. In March 2022, just four years after they arrive, they tell Cromwell parishioners that they've accepted a call to Mount Maunganui, near Tauranga. They leave two months later.

MORE NEEDS TO BE SAID ABOUT DOUGLAS'S RELATIVELY short tenure as minister. For much of Douglas's time in Cromwell and several months after he leaves, Douglas does an excellent job supervising a young intern minister, Ryan Feng. Ryan is Chinese, speaks better English than a good number of Kiwis, has a warm, outgoing personality, grounds his preaching in the Bible but also in everyday life, and speaks like he absolutely believes every word he's saying—and he does.

Ryan begins at Cromwell in January 2000, having approached Douglas in 2019. His three-year internship has challenges aplenty. He experiences the bluntness of some in the congregation during COVID, but his weekly meetings with Douglas help him through this. Mervyn Mitchell, recently retired from his role as Session Clerk, chairs a 'Ministry Reflection Group' which is a requirement for Presbyterian interns, and also helpful for Ryan. He appreciates the empathy Douglas Bradley shows towards him, as exemplified by the special farewell dinner Douglas and Judy put on for Ryan and his wife, Tara, when the internship is complete. Ryan respects Douglas's ability to keep Presbytery at arms' length by turning down requests to be on committees, commissions and the like so that he can concentrate on the battle in Cromwell.

Ryan now has his hands full as the minister of the Bishopdale Presbyterian Church in Christchurch. As we chat over coffee in a Bishopdale café, he is wistful about leaving Cromwell, necessary though it was for him under the rules for interns. Pastoral care efforts for the parish are led selflessly by Edith Geddis and are effective, especially for older church members, but Ryan sees so much more that could be done. In his mind, reaching out to poorer people has got to be more than just a regular but modest contribution to the local Foodbank. When the middle-aged brother and sister drive their car in behind the church and sleep in it for several nights, it prompts lively debate in Session. This couple had lost a profitable small business and their home. Surely the church would help them? Well, yes, Session Clerk Mervyn Mitchell contacts welfare authorities and arranges benefits and accommodation. But where is the ongoing service to the increasing number of poorer people in Cromwell?

After the Fengs and the Bradleys leave, Cromwell is yet again in need of 'stated supply'. Reverend Peter Eaton, a retired Baptist minister living in Wanaka, contributes generously on a casual basis several times. Most recently, there are two continuous longer periods of ministry which are in the hands of two fine and unforgettable men: Pastor Alan Wilkinson—yes, the man who organised the quick-build of the new church in 2006—and Rev Dr Tony Martin.

Alan's role in the quick-build of the new church is pivotal. If we gave out knighthoods at CPC, he'd certainly have one, and now he's back—you guessed it—as 'stated supply' in Cromwell for twelve weeks in the first half of 2023. Alan's preaching style is unique. He has notes and he does know where he wants to go with the sermon, but he frequently walks away from his notes on the lectern and speaks from the heart for two, three, four or more minutes, then somehow finds his way back to the notes and the original plan, mostly. His warmth, his sense of urgency for the church, and his unfailing commitment to the Christian way are compelling.

Not so well known in Cromwell is that Alan and Yvonne Wilkinson have also been missionaries to Malaysia and particularly, to Myanmar. Their Myanmar involvement begins in 1995 when they are pastoring the Levin Apostolic Church. That church's mission group is looking for an unreached people group[55] to support. Alan makes his first trip to Myanmar that year. Soon afterwards, the Wilkinsons move to Cromwell, but their connection with Myanmar continues, with regular visits to provide ongoing financial, practical and spiritual support to the new church they're working with. The church there wants to develop a Bible school, an orphanage, and a pre-school for their local communities. Alan's practical knowledge, skills and abilities as a pastor and builder, and Yvonne's as a pre-school teacher, can be used by God in the process.

It takes twenty years for the dream to become reality, but it happens. For most of 2016, Alan and Yvonne go to Myanmar for a number of months to physically support the construction of a six-storey building that will house the church, pre-school, and primary school. During this time, they're regularly involved in church life on Sundays. Alan is project manager and overall quality controller to ensure the building is fit for purpose. His task is to plan, design, organise, manage and motivate local workers, plus to work hands-on as and when needed. Yvonne supplies practical support and resources for the development of the pre-school. She works with an interpreter to provide parent education and teacher training. She also takes classes in music

---

55 A phrase used to describe people who haven't heard about Jesus Christ and the Christian faith.

and movement, and story times in English, with both pre-school and older school children.

After a brief stint back in New Zealand, they return to Myanmar the following year, 2017, for a further six months to see the building finished, and again in 2018, when Alan's building expertise is needed to finish an incomplete area. Yvonne uses the opportunity to run a teacher-training course, opening it up to pre-school teachers outside the church community over three successive Saturdays. The Wilkinsons are excited to see the ongoing development and growth of the church, pre-school, and school.

Five years later, in 2023, they make another visit, their first since the military takeover. This time, Alan's focus is on church leadership training, providing a leaders' and elders' seminar, and attending an ordination service for new pastors. Yvonne leads some pre-school training; the school's closure for over two years has led to significant staff changes. Both preach on Sundays. The biggest privilege is to attend the celebrations for the release of the pastor's daughter, who has been imprisoned for two years for helping Christian friends who refuse to go back to work for the military. It's very encouraging to see the school and pre-school getting back into action with a full roll and happy children and parents.

Eventually, Alan and Yvonne return to New Zealand and take on yet another challenge: pastoring a New Life Church in Gore, Eastern Southland. But perhaps there's unfinished work to be done in Asia . . .

THE REV DR TONY MARTIN'S CAREER IN MINISTRY IS unlike that of any other. He has served for a long period as a chaplain in the British Army, including in trouble spots like Northern Ireland and the Balkans. Widely appreciated and respected for his work alongside front-line soldiers, he later becomes the senior chaplain in NATO, based in Germany, with the provisional rank of Lieutenant-Colonel.

When Tony returns permanently to New Zealand in 2005, he's shocked to discover that in Southland, where he'd started as a Presbyterian minister in the 1980s, numbers are down from twenty-one full-time Presbyterian ministers in 1989 to only four or five. He recognises that the church-style parades, in which chaplains play a key part, have made his wife Katherine and him inclined towards Anglican liturgy and worship service structure. In his autobiography, *An Extraordinary Journey*, he notes,

> *"We both valued liturgy, traditional alongside contemporary music, and a reflective approach to worship."*

Tony becomes an Anglican priest in 2019—well, to be more accurate, an 'Honorary Non-Stipendiary Priest Assistant'. This can be loosely translated as 'unpaid bloke up the front helping the others'. Then he adds another title to his already impressive collection, taking on a full-time role for twelve months as 'Priest Missioner' for the widespread Taieri and Otago Peninsula parish. Thence to retirement briefly, before taking up the 'stated supply' role in Cromwell.

He serves CPC well for almost a year, bringing his caravan up from East Taieri where he and Katherine live. Each week, he stays in the caravan from Sunday to Wednesday, then returns home until the wee hours of the following Sunday, when he has the road to Cromwell pretty much to himself, always arriving in plenty of time for the 9 am service. This long service to Cromwell enables the even longer search for a new minister to reach a positive conclusion. Tony's contribution to CPC will be remembered for years to come.

Ministry and Mission

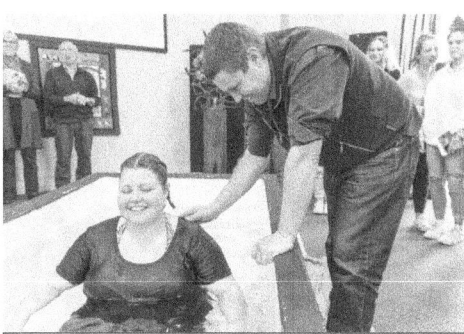

Phoebe Harrington's baptism by her dad, Jim

Thai Team 2012, Murray Robertson, Rob Pendreigh, Laura Winstanley, Lane Coughlan, Wayne Bell. Emma Pendreigh in front

10th Cromwell Charity Ball, 2016

Fish & Chips Missions Tea, 1992. Old Church Hall. D & S Caldwell 2nd row, Shirley in white.

Family Camp, 2009 En Hakkore

Douglas Bradley, Minister 2018-22, and his wife Judy

Mae Chaem Hostel, Thailand

Cathy Mann, Trish Copland, Kelly Keenan

Ryan Feng taking goods to Foodbank, 2021 (COVID times)

Catherine Forsyth and a mix of singers

The Geustyn Family, New Zealand citizens

Alastair and Krisztina Hansen, missionaries to Hungary, and their children, Jake and Lili.

Seven Cromwellians and sixteen
Zambians, 2019

Johnstones in Niger, 2020

Youth Group ski day, 2021

The Young Family, home after
15 years in Malawi

Daniel and Anita
Muir with Priscilla

Malcolm & Sandy Potter,
missionaries to Thailand

Clarissa Bochel, helper of
Cambodian women

CHAPTER ELEVEN

More Missionaries Who Went Out

AFTER CPC'S BEGINNINGS IN THE 1870S, IT TAKES ninety years before its first missionary is 'commissioned'. This means the church promises to support, financially and in other useful ways, a missionary going out to work in a Christian role in a foreign country.[56] This includes a good number who have no direct link to Cromwell during their service overseas.

Beryl Anderson (nee Beaton) goes to the tiny Cromwell District High School, 1951-1955. There are only forty kids there then. It's a shock when in 1956, she's sent to Southland Girls' High School, her mum's old school, for there are forty girls in her class alone!

In May 1964, Beryl goes to the New Hebrides as a registered nurse at Vaemali Hospital, Epi, for seventeen months. This means lots of public health work, walking around the island giving vaccinations. Beryl resigns in late 1965, then in May 1966, she

---

56   See Appendix 2: Members and Adherents Serving Overseas

marries Doug Anderson, a bachelor Presbyterian minister. He serves as minister at Woodville from 1964-68 before they bid farewell to New Zealand and leave by boat for Singapore and Malaysia, where they will serve for the next thirteen years.

Libby Smith (nee Sutton) works for Presbyterian Missions as charge nurse of a mission hospital in Tongoa in the New Hebrides. Back in New Zealand, she's commissioned for overseas service by the Coromandel Presbyterian Parish in February 1970. Returning to the New Hebrides, she serves at Paton Memorial Hospital, Vila, in 1970 and at the Silimauri Health Centre, Tongoa, in 1970.

Some years later, Libby does theological training and becomes minister at St Stevens, Kurow, where pastors have included former cabinet minister Rev Sir Arnold Nordmeyer and Cromwell minister Rev Doug Stout. Then, she does ministry work in Cromwell. In her late sixties, she marries John Smith. She retires in her early seventies and dies in 2023.

Rev Robert Patterson is supply minister for Cromwell-Arrowtown, from March 1974 to April 1975. In February 1976, he becomes a lecturer in Old Testament at the Theological College of Eastern Indonesia. He serves twenty-four years there, finishing in 1999. Robert publishes many Bible commentaries and other books in the Indonesian language, as well as two church histories, *A History of the Pukerau Presbyterian Church,* 1962 and *Cromwell & Districts Presbyterian Church: 100 years 1875-1975.* He dies at Ross Home, Dunedin, in June 2024, aged ninety.

Alan and Edith Buxton's Vanuatu wanderings begin with a Youth With A Mission trip to the Island of Ambyrm, one of the less accessible volcanic islands. This is a water-collection project, mostly supplying and helping to fit spouting. It makes them aware of life's difficulties on Pacific islands and the poverty in our own back yard. Much more important is their becoming aware of Vanuatu life. It helps them to welcome Ni Van seasonal workers coming to Cromwell and to soften the culture shock the first groups of workers experience.

Alan is approached by Onehunga One Tree Hill Rotary Club to assist with wastewater upgrades at a regional hospital—an old Church of England Mission Hospital at Lolowai, Ambae Island. The newly independent Vanuatu Government lacks the finances to maintain infrastructural assets—roads, schools, communication, shipping, and airports. Lolowai Hospital is one such asset. This is a major project, involving much concrete cutting and breaking to install new under-floor pipework, hand-trenching using local labour, and construction of a massive septic tank and drainage field. Simultaneously, other team members build new toilet and shower blocks in the existing three wards, replacing cracking concrete and wooden walls. This work is mostly done by training and paying local tradesmen.

Rotary International's massive financial clout covers the cost. Club members handle the purchase and transport of materials, a very fraught process. Harder still, they negotiate the political web to get work approvals. (Church of England Bishop, government, Ministry of Health, village chiefs, hospital administration, and a myriad of others have to agree and give approval.)

Alan makes five trips to Ambae. Edith comes on three of these, spending time on women's groups, preschools, tourism training of girls and general health promotion. Alan comments:

"All our trips are great—genuine cultural experiences, some amazing, some grim. We never get malaria or dengue fever but meet lots of mosquitos. We eat some of the best food ever, but don't recommend roast fruit bat."

Malcolm (a.k.a. Pottsy) and Sandy Potter are involved in Cromwell Presbyterian Church life for sixteen years before they go off as missionaries to Chiang Mai in Northern Thailand in early 2001. They've held leadership positions in the church as youth leaders and as elders, and Malcolm has been Session Clerk for a period. They do a short-term trip to Thailand in 1996, and this further whets their appetite for mission work. They've also been active in the support team for Jim and Helen Harrington, who go out in 1990 to Africa.

There is intensity about these two; no half-measures about their faith. That said, they find the two years of language learning painful when they first go to Thailand. The huge alphabet is a particular challenge. But they do well. The present author and his wife visit the Potters in early 2014 and have the privilege of seeing Sandy bartering with sellers in the local produce market, with much banter and laughter which signals both Sandy's mastery of the language and a good relationship between the locals and the foreign missionaries. Very impressive!

Pottsy and Sandy separately arrive at the conclusion that God is calling them very clearly to build a hostel at Mae Chaem—a two-hour drive west from Chiang Mai, over a winding hill road. The objective is to provide Christian accommodation for hill-tribe teenagers attending a nearby state high school. Generous and unexpected funding turning up when there is no other significant support for the project seems to be confirmation of Pottsy and Sandy's vision: for example, a Christchurch couple follow the biblical command to tithe[57] to the project, and then, just for good measure, they give a second large donation.

If you're not from a Christian background, the next part of the Potters' story may be difficult to get your head around. After many years of the hostel operating, the Potters experience what they come to recognise as a demonic attack. Two new couples come to the hostel to trial as adult supervisors for three months. The older couple become harshly critical of the younger couple, and through deception turn the majority of the teenagers in the hostel against the younger, godly supervisors. This results in twenty-five out of the thirty-three hostel teenagers choosing to leave. In response to a God-given strategy, Pottsy, the remaining staff and students march around the buildings seven times. They sense that "God is raising the roofs and filling them with His glory," and a demon is seen leaving. Over time, the numbers of resident students begins to increase once again.

Christians obviously believe in the power of God, the power of prayer, and the resurrection of the dead. Not so well known is that they also believe in the powers of evil, such as demons, as in Potters' story in the paragraph above. In the book of Ephesians in the New Testament, we read:

> *Our struggle is not against flesh and blood, but against the rulers, against the powers of this dark world, against the spiritual forces of evil in the heavenly realms.*
>
> *Ephesians 6:12*

---

57   Tithe: to give ten percent of one's income.

When hostel occupants finish high school, some go on to tertiary study. The Potters work with Donald and Suzanne Lewis from Dunedin to set up a small female hostel near the university that the girls attend in Chiang Mai.

There are several visitors to Thailand to carry out specific practical tasks and to support and encourage the Potters in their work. One of these visits, in 2013-14, involved Murray Robertson, Rob Pendreigh (CPC's minister at the time), Laura Winstanley, Lane Coughlan, Wayne Bell, and Emma Pendreigh. Murray Robertson filed this report about this trip:

> *"Months of planning and fund-raising: a garage sale and a book called 'Satisfied' (made up of recipes from the congregation). Proceeds go towards travel costs for the younger team members. Our base is the Mae Chaem Hostel. We travel to Yot Pai Village, staying the night in a home perched on the side of a hill—sleeping under mosquito nets while listening to the animals outside. The local Pastor Panya travels around ministering on a motorbike. A highlight is praying for a young child—you can feel the Holy Spirit move amongst us.*
>
> *Next day, we start our projects in Mae Chaem: Rob, teaching and ministering to the young people in the hostel; pastoral oversight of the team and general dogsbody; Wayne, installing water tanks and irrigation. Lane, his joinery skills improve hostel storage areas; Laura and Emma, teaching English, running games, painting buildings, leading worship for hostel services; Murray, welding and repairing steel bunks; building a queen-sized bed for Ma'am and Prasert; building*

a shelter for the outside gas cooker; making a rhythm stick out of bottle tops; teaching the harmonica.

Much of the work requires adapting: what would be simple in New Zealand can be difficult in Thailand e.g., it's hard to find a broom, then the handle won't fit, so shaping with a machete is required. It's wonderful to see what Malcolm and Sandy have established and to be part of a mission that makes a difference to the lives of the people we have contact with."

Today, the hostel is thriving. The Potters have come home to Cromwell after twenty years of devoted service. A job well done.

OVER A FIFTEEN-YEAR PERIOD BETWEEN 2005 AND 2019, Clarissa Bochel makes yearly trips with Mercy Ministries Foundation (MMF) to work among children and HIV-AIDS sufferers in Thailand and Cambodia. Here's an edited diary of her work:

"After a tsunami in Thailand's south, I go in May 2005 to help local Christians build a 'cement' family home. Then I travel to Poipet, Cambodia, a town with families displaced by the Khmer Rouge. At the MMF school in the slums, I meet a man who wants to build a hospice—with bamboo stilts and floors, rubber walls and a grass roof—for HIV/ AIDS single mums. I vow I'll return to work on this project. Before going home that July, I volunteer at a home for lost tsunami children . . .

. . . Home for three months before returning to Poipet in October 2005. No progress yet on the AIDS Hospice. I'm asked by a local NGO to open a restaurant for Christian teams. I train three ex-prostitutes in Western cooking. Two of these girls now work in top Thai restaurants; the third has become a Christian, is married, and is a staff member at Happy Home. There are three MMF ministries around Poipet: the Hope Centre for HIV single women (some with children) twenty kilometres out of town; the children's Happy Home School (orphanage for forty kids) in town; the informal 'top up' pre-school (four hundred kids) in [a tough local] slum. I return to New Zealand in April 2006.

. . . Only two months home this time, then back to Poipet in June 2006. The Hope Centre is now up and running. I do vocational training, teaching girls to sew for businesses in New Zealand (like Postie Plus). Sitting at a sewing machine all day when you have HIV and only weigh around forty kilograms isn't easy, so we soon change to a knitting program. This also gives the girls freedom to work around the compound and care for their kids, and it only needs a few pairs of needles. I buy yarn in Wanaka. The hats they make in Poipet sell on the open market in Canada and the USA. This means these women can earn $US10 a day—much better than fifty cents a day for hauling pigs across the Mekong River. Some give their hearts to Jesus. I get home to New Zealand after seven months away, in January 2007.

In 2008, I manage a children's home for tsunami orphans in Phang Nga (South Thailand) for seven months. Between

2008 and 2013, I return, normally in June each year, for seven to nine months to help at the Hope Centre. In 2013, Hope Centre closes, so I join the Happy Home team, looking after children and teaching life skills to both them and the staff. I'm also asked to do a task like this at the MMF Happy Home in Chiang Saen, Northern Thailand. So, nine months each year is split between the two homes. All funds raised go to help kids who leave for further studies. These trips continue until 2019.

In 2021, I link into an online market opportunity in Queenstown. As an NGO, MMF doesn't provide for staff retirement, so I train two staff at Chiang Saen to use electric sewing machines and overlockers provided from New Zealand. This project is now providing funds for a retirement account. Over the last fifteen years, I've been privileged to be part of these homes with the children and staff. Many in their villages come to know Jesus. It's been a joy to watch them grow and 'be set free'. I thought God sent me on this journey to teach, love, empower and encourage. Little did I know how much more He had in store for me. I have learnt it's about relying on Him. Asia is where my heart is . . ."

Alastair and Krisztina Hansen leave with their children Lili and Jake to live in Hungary in October 2019. Alastair is to coach baseball in Erd[58], help erect a giant indoor practice facility, lead a youth group for players known as 'Three Strikes'—fun, fellowship and food—and assist short-term mission teams.

---

58   Pronounced 'Eared'.

In late 2020, they move to Tata to help a Finnish couple, Jarmo and Pirjo, minister amongst Roma people—running after-school clubs, Sunday School programmes and camps. They also help foreign short-term mission teams. As a first-language speaker, Krisztina is vital to this work, interpreting in meetings, with kids and between locals and visiting foreign teams. This helps develop relationships with kids and parents in all our programmes. In 2021, Alastair is made head of Operation Mobilisation's sports ministry in Hungary; he begins looking for new ministries to start there.

When the Ukraine war breaks out, they assist refugees who come to Tata to acclimatise. Krisztina's language knowledge is again vital; Slovakian is similar to Ukrainian.

From May-August 2022, the Hansens are on furlough. In 2023, a new Roma couple come to lead the Roma ministry. The Hansens begin a new sports ministry in a mainly Roma school, running this until they leave Hungary and return permanently to New Zealand in January 2024.

CHAPTER TWELVE

The Cromwell of Today

AT THE TIME OF WRITING IN 2024, CROMWELL IS SIX to seven times the size it was in 1975. In 2019, Statistics NZ declared Cromwell to be the fastest-growing urban locality in New Zealand! There have been major demographic and social changes, inevitably, in the wake of such population growth. After the dam opened in 1993, there was a lull, but soon, growth resumed. The Cromwell College roll in its first year, 1978, was under two hundred; today, it's pushing seven hundred, and thus able to offer more of the academic, cultural and recreational opportunities that boarding schools have long used as a drawcard for Cromwell students, especially in Years 11-13.

Cromwell is nowadays identified as a desirable place for people to retire to, especially from Southland, coastal Otago and Canterbury. There are also more refugees from Auckland who've discovered that there are better things to be found this far south of the Bombay Hills. Real estate is cheaper than in Queenstown and Wanaka, but in late 2024, the average selling price of a Cromwell house is around $920,000—and it's been higher than that. Once the poor cousin of Wanaka, Queenstown, Arrowtown and Alexandra, Cromwell nowadays sells more and more properties for over two million dollars.

Roughly equidistant from Queenstown and Wanaka and just twenty-three kilometres from Clyde and thirty-two kilometres from Alexandra, Cromwell is the true geographical centre of Central Otago. Increasingly, businesses base themselves here to service the whole region. All of this means a thriving and very competitive building industry. The local giveaway news sheet, The Bulletin, recently had seventeen builders' advertisements in it. There are also sixteen jobs advertised. Most employers say finding employees locally is hard.

There was some disappointment in Cromwell when the Mall opened in 1985—did the town fight hard enough to get it near the highway where it was before the dam was built? But shopping is quite a bit better than in the 70s, even if it still lags behind Queenstown in the range and number of megastores to choose from. There's real choice in accommodation and there are plenty of eating out options now. Some of us used to shoot rabbits down the uninhabited McNulty Road in the late 70s, but today, it has business enterprises or residential properties on both sides for virtually all of its 1.7-kilometre length.

Cromwell people do still plan shopping in Frankton, but we're more likely to combine this with other reasons for going there, such as meeting people at the airport or seeing medical specialists. We're less likely to shop in Queenstown itself; traffic snarl-ups between Frankton and Queenstown make that less attractive, and prices tend to be higher. The Cromwell-Frankton road is also very busy, especially at the beginning and end of the day.

CPC mightn't be as diverse as city congregations, but it *is* much more cosmopolitan than it used to be. There's been a good few South African families coming and going, reflecting the post-apartheid exodus and also their search to find the right jobs and the right place to settle down in New Zealand. One CPC elder is Tongan. There's a Scottish family. Vanuatuan men have been coming for twenty years to work on vineyards and cherry orchards, for up to seven months each year. When they're in town, a steady stream of these men attend the Sunday 10:30 am service. In the first few years they came, CPC's own Alan Buxton did a terrific job as a sort of unofficial liaison and welfare officer. The wider Cromwell community is similarly more multicultural: there are Sri Lankan and Filipina nurses in the two rest homes, Golden View and Ripponburn.

Most CPC churchgoers are normal Kiwis. Plenty have special talents, but they don't think that those gifts make them more important or better than others. They are outward-looking, doing their bit to contribute to New Zealand society as a whole, not inward-looking, just doing 'church stuff'. Now or in the last generation or so, CPC people are or have been:

- Local-body politicians in the now-much-larger Cromwell, which came with the Clyde hydroelectric dam.
- Contributors of skills to the workforce that built that dam.

- Polling-place managers and vote counters in more than one general election.
- Farmers, including leaders in agricultural innovation: a new breed of sheep—for which stock numbers are growing rapidly—bred by a church family.
- Proprietors of a leading car servicing and sales business.
- A director of a geotech firm.
- Brilliantly creative inventor of walnut farming devices and designer of Cromwell's iconic fruit sculpture at the main entrance to the town.
- Sports men and women—golfers across the handicap range; senior rugby and cricket players; coaches and administrators at every level up to national; provincially-ranked indoor bowlers and hockey reps.
- Volunteers who've given hours in all kinds of capacities e.g., musicians, cooking for large groups including catering for funerals; men in the local night-watch patrol; leader of a project to build a community hall and service rooms.
- Responsible objectors who stand up for what they believe in a public setting.
- Two Justices of the Peace.
- A lawyer in a local firm.
- Doctors and senior nurses.
- Winners of prestigious prizes for university courses.

- Leaders of national charitable initiatives: the first leader of the World Vision 40 Hour Famine in New Zealand.
- The single negotiator persuading McDonald's restaurants to open the first Ronald McDonald House for parents of children with life-threatening illnesses (Nov 1987).
- Principals and teachers in all kinds of schools in New Zealand and around the world: single-sex and co-ed, private and state, rural and urban, small and large, multi-cultural and mono-cultural. This includes some really tough schools, which so badly need teachers who do the *mahi*,[59] cut the mustard, lead the students towards maturity.

Cromwell Presbyterian Church isn't vastly bigger in 2024 than at the turn of the century. It's doing well to keep numbers up: like other mainline churches, many Presbyterian churches closed or amalgamated in recent years. Social and demographic change is part of this, but not the whole story. As Kate Borrie, a long-standing member here in Cromwell, declares, "It's counter-cultural to be a Christian today." Nevertheless, there's a buzz about Cromwell Presbyterian Church in 2024 which indicates life and warmth amongst its people.

In an age when schools are no longer willing—for whatever reasons—to host the Bible-in-Schools programme, CPC tries hard to connect with young families. Mainly Music, previously known as Rhythm and Dance, is a programme for pre-school children

---

59 Māori word, meaning 'work'.

that gives young mothers a great activity for their littlies to be part of; it's also a chance for young mums to socialise. It first sprang into life in Cromwell under the leadership of Diane Young in the late nineties, and since then, Jan Stanton and her team of helpers have ensured its continuing success. Jan deservedly receives complimentary letters and profuse messages of thanks from mums who appreciate this programme which so enriches the lives of their littlies.

Sunday School is still the continuity programme for children in CPC, but it battles against the busyness of modern life—both parents working, the demands of sport and other activities. Sunday in times past was undoubtedly that day widely recognised as primarily for church life, including Sunday School, but not anymore. Finding people within the church who'll commit to being there every Sunday to teach Sunday School is a challenge, too. Men don't seem comfortable there—a striking parallel, perhaps, with the fall in the number of men entering Early Years and Primary teaching.

There are two annual events hosted by CPC which attract many children from around the town. Catherine Cowie, a Catholic friend and long-standing Cromwell resident, comments that CPC sets an example for the other churches by reaching out to children through these programmes.

Held on 31 October, the Light Party is a Christian alternative to Halloween. For many Christians, the primary concern with Halloween is its perceived association with paganism and the occult. Hence the idea of Light—the light and freedom which comes with faith in Jesus Christ—as opposed to the darkness and fear found in paganism and the occult. The Light Party offers fun activities and good food for adults and children alike, and no knocking on doors to offer a 'trick or treat' option.

In the same vein, Santa Land is an enticing festival of Christmas events taking over the church complex for three days every December. As its name suggests, it includes the secular Santa traditions, but also the nativity story so central to the Christian faith. Hundreds come through the church for this event every year, mainly but not only young families.

Youth activities in 2024 are in the hands of Cathy Mann and Trish Copland. Like most country towns, Cromwell is always in need of healthy activities for teenagers, although it's much better off in 2024 than in past generations. Cathy is a stayer—she has served in the area of children and youth work for many years now. Trish is a vital connecting influence with the local college because she's a staff member there.

A key influence in many current CPC initiatives is Mandi Geustyn who came to Cromwell from South Africa in 2017 to become CPC's Children's and Families Worker.

> *"I'd completed a degree in Christian children's counselling but didn't expect it would get me a job and get our family to New Zealand. In South Africa, no one pays you to work for a church. You don't do ministry for payment. It's not about money."*

She stops and smiles, a touch of puzzlement lingering on her face.

> *"I still have difficulty reconciling being paid and working for God."*

It needs to be said here that both the Central Lakes Trust and the Presbyterian Synod made Mandi's job possible with generous funding. The difference in Sunday School and young families programmes has been spectacular.

Several months after Mandi arrives and after the seemingly standard battle with New Zealand immigration, her husband, Jason, and their children Leané and Xander come from South Africa to join her. Jason is a highly-skilled engineer but can't get employment in his field in Cromwell, so finds a job in Timaru, three and a half hours away by car! These early years in New Zealand certainly have their stresses for the Geustyn family, but God is good: Jason gets a job in Cromwell which at least means they can be together; the job will do for now, even though it's not the best fit with his past skills and experience. Not surprisingly, he's moved up into a more fulfilling role in recent times. Mandi recounts:

"Jason and I were born in the same hospital, four days apart. He grew up in a church family: his Dad was the equivalent of Session Clerk, and his Mum, the Sunday School superintendent. I didn't go to church. I'd go sometimes to Sunday School with friends after sleepovers. I was twenty-eight when I came to faith. Jason and I had been married for five years. We were dating at twenty/twenty-one. Married at twenty-three. Leané was born when we were twenty-four."

There's an independent streak in this family to admire. It's not just stubbornness; it's an unwavering commitment to the biblical model of Christian living. Church is for every Sunday, not just if you're not busy that day.

"You wear good clothes to church, not to be fashionable but to honour God. Can't go with the shorts-and-jandals look at church. That's what we wear down by the lake . . ."

And for much the same reasons, Mandi pleads for taking communion more seriously:

"The Lord's Supper isn't understood—it's just a habit—the Christian thing to do. Everyone does it. A deeper connection is needed. We should pray about it the day before. Don't take it until and unless you're ready. Be there to be part of the celebration of it, and to truly draw closer to God."

Four years after coming to New Zealand, Mandi is head-hunted by the Presbyterian Synod to oversee children's and families' work in all Presbyterian churches in Otago and Southland, with special responsibility for the Messy Church programme. She still lives in Cromwell, and she and her family make a huge contribution to all aspects of church life. "It's what Christians do, isn't it?" she asks. She and Jason worry about the future of the church in Cromwell, whatever its strengths. "Who will follow the current leaders?" they ask, almost simultaneously. There's a big age gap in the middle of the church demographic. "The same people are doing just about everything!" They chatter animatedly about how things must change.

"We're used to a very traditional Dutch Reformed service. Men stand up while they're praying; women stay seated. Kids grow up used to staying seated in the service, saying the Lord's Prayer and the Apostles Creed. No rosters; you're the Sunday School teacher every Sunday. Even if there are

visitors, don't waste the opportunity. God doesn't have holidays!

For years, Grandma's been praying for me. Her house was spartan—no TV, Scripture verses on the wall, rules for everything. When I told her I'd become a Christian, she said God told her the mantle of children's ministry would fall on my shoulders. Grandparents should never underestimate their prayers!

Faith at home is a key factor. This normalises faith. Fellowship brings Christians together. God doesn't put us all in one church by mistake. There's still a huge need for volunteer hours. Jason and I want to help with mundane tasks. You have to be intentional about including your kids. Kids need to look up to older Christians—that's why it's important for Xander to play guitar with Murray (Robertson).

Parents aren't bringing kids to Sunday School in New Zealand. It's their responsibility. Church should be not negotiable. If you bring your child to church, they'll learn how to be volunteers. Do we give them tasks in which they can serve? They don't even know what Session is or what the elders do."

Kiwis can learn from this family's experience. Their first language is Afrikaans, so they understand the language challenges faced by New Zealand missionaries going abroad. It's hard to 'think and speak in English'—and New Zealand English has a slang very different from the English they learned in South Africa. The lack of discipline in some classes at the local school, and a world view far from their own, leads Jason and Mandi to a big decision: Xander is home-schooled now. Leané and Xander have their own active Christian faith, which means standing on their own feet among increasingly secular peers.

Leané is now doing teacher training in Dunedin. She quickly realises that little room is left in the programme for her to disagree about matters of culture, ethics, gender and morals. She's done a placement at a local Christian school and thinks she'd like to teach in a school like that when she graduates. Every Sunday, she travels across Dunedin—about ninety minutes each way—to a church in Leith Valley where she feels at home.

They don't miss the high fences and burglar bars that surround many urban homes in South Africa. They do value the many good aspects of New Zealand life they're experiencing. Jason and Xander have recently been to Dunedin to watch a rugby test. Xander already has a single-figure golf handicap. There's a warmth and vitality about this family which is almost infectious. But "material things do nothing for our salvation!" declare Jason and Mandi, in near-unison. "We must not forget to depend on God!"

You can almost hear the echo from the Psalms:

I will lift up my eyes unto the hills. Where does my help come from? From the Lord, who made heaven and earth!
Psalm 121:1-2

CHAPTER THIRTEEN

The Newcomer Experience

WHAT IS IT LIKE FOR A NEWCOMER TO GO TO A Cromwell church service in 2024? There are two services most Sundays, at 9 am and 10:30 am, with morning tea in between, mainly for those who've been at the earlier service. Those arriving for the 10:30 event are welcome to line up if they didn't have their morning coffee fix before they left home.

As a newcomer, I'm not sure what to expect. Others have arrived for the 9 am service before me: the minister, the duty elder[60], the duty manager[61], and the organist. Today, Helen Harrington is rostered to play.

Dress is mostly tidy informal, although some guys run to jacket and tie. Really, no rules about what you wear. At the door,

---

60 One of the church leaders.

61 One of the group that looks after the building and other business aspects of the church.

I'm met by a greeter who says hi to people as they arrive. There's often a brief personal chat—just as we might have if we bumped into each other in the supermarket—but now, the greeter gives me a copy of the weekly newsletter. Inside, the duty elder spots me quickly as a visitor, and we have a brief and warm chat. The contact details of key church leaders are in the newsletter, and it also advertises upcoming church events. For example, a youth group notice for a carwash next Saturday to raise funds for their annual camp because cost will be an issue for some who want to go.

This 9 am service is in the Lowburn Chapel, just off the main foyer. Lots of history here. There used to be a Presbyterian Church at Lowburn, a small settlement about five kilometres north of Cromwell on the road to Wanaka. Services there were like the one I'm going into now—traditional, like they've been for several centuries, but less formal.

There are two stained-glass windows at the front, brought from the old Cromwell Church when this one was built in 2006-2007. One of these is a memorial to Captain W D Jolly, a church leader who died in France in World War One. There's also a beautifully fashioned communion table made by another member, Bob Miller, who died about ten years ago. This little chapel is contained within the larger church building, but it has its own character. It's a special link to those who were part of the church in times past.

As I enter the chapel, I'm given 'The Purple Book', a more modern version of the hymn books used by churches for centuries past.[62] I sit next to Fiti Vou, a smiling Samoan man. Fiti, I discover, married a Kiwi and they live in a nearby retirement village. The

---

62 There's also the 'Red Book', an A5 folder with extra hymns/songs compiled locally.

Lowburn Chapel holds about sixty people and has comfortable individual chairs, not like the bench pews of yesteryear which had no cushioning and caused plenty of wriggles as services went on. The room is warm; it needs to be because a good few of those present are pensioners and below-zero temperatures are common here at nine o'clock in the winter.

The organ is playing in the minutes preceding the service. Some sit quietly, perhaps praying, listening to the music or just reflecting on the week past. There's a low buzz of conversation, too; again, no rigid rules—people are relaxed and pleased to see each other. Just before 9 am, the person leading the service comes in. Today, it's Ann-Marie Leyser. A Cromwellian all her life, with her husband John, she's worked hard on their orchard for many years. She welcomes us all, then gives the 'Call to Worship'—a short passage from the Bible that helps us put aside the everyday things we might have on our minds and concentrate on deeper stuff.

> *The LORD is the everlasting God; He created the entire world. He never grows tired or weary . . . He strengthens those who are weak and tired. Even those who are young grow weak; young people can fall exhausted. But those who trust in the LORD for help will find their strength renewed. They'll rise on wings like eagles; they'll run and not get weary; they'll walk and not grow weak.*
>
> *Isaiah 40:28-31 GNT*

Next, we stand to sing the first hymn: *Now Thank We All Our God*. I see that this was written almost four hundred years ago by a guy called Martin Rinkart, then translated into English (only two hundred years ago!) by Catherine Winkworth.[63] It's not in hopelessly dated English; those present obviously know and like this song. Although fewer than forty people are present, they sing with gusto and with more than a hint of harmony:

> *Who from our mothers' arms, has blessed us on our way*
> *With countless gifts of love, and still is ours, today!*

We sit again, and I get a real surprise. Ann-Marie picks up a basket, which, it turns out, is full of small, separately-wrapped pieces of chocolate. "Who's had a birthday or an anniversary?" she asks. "He has!" a voice from somewhere behind me says. Turning, I realise it's a grinning wife forcing her husband to admit he's just had a birthday. He's duly rewarded with a small Crunchie bar and doesn't look displeased with his better half. Someone else says their grand-daughter has just played rugby for Otago (how times have changed!) and that's worth a selection from the chocolate basket, too.

Church notices then appear on a screen. This place is anything but idle, it seems. The youth group carwash features, as does the impending arrival of a new minister. Regular events in church life are also there: the monthly Evergreens Communion Service—for oldies, really—and Two-Course Tuesday, providing a cooked lunch every fortnight for just fifteen dollars a head. Reminders, too, about exercise, indoor bowls, prayer and Bible study groups. We also hear about 'Messy Church', a very informal church service wrapped around a shared evening meal. Suits young families, is free, and everyone is welcome.

---

63 *Now Thank We All Our God*, Martin Rinkart, 1936, public domain.

The next hymn is *I Heard The Voice Of Jesus Say*.[64] Different, this, with a catchy change of key. Again, well-known. Written by an English clergyman nearly one hundred and eighty years ago, which could easily have put me off, but it still seems to fit today ...

> *I came to Jesus as I was, weary and worn and sad;*
> *I found in Him a resting place, and He has made me glad ...*
> *I looked to Jesus and I found, in Him my Star, my Sun;*
> *And in that light of life I'll walk, till travelling days are done.*

Prayers are next. I soon realise that Edith Geddis, the retired doctor leading the prayers, has a real empathy for the hurts and needs of others. She prays especially for those caught up in things they can't control: the wars in Gaza and the Ukraine; the elderly, sick and unemployed people in New Zealand and elsewhere. She prays for those who volunteer to work amongst needy people; she prays for young people everywhere; she prays fervently for justice. Can't argue with any of that.

Bible readings follow. They're an insert in the newsletter, so we can all follow what's being read, and/or come back to the reading during the sermon.

We sing again. Not as rousing as the first two, but with no less feeling:

> *He is Lord, He is Lord, He has risen from the dead, and He*
> *is Lord;*
> *Every knee shall bow, every tongue confess, that Jesus Christ*
> *is Lord!*[65]

---

64 *I Heard the Voice of Jesus Say*, Horatius Bonar, 1846, public domain.
65 *He Is Lord, He is Lord*, attributed to Steve Vest, public domain.

Some these days struggle with 'thee' and 'thou' language but it doesn't seem to matter to those here. Thumbing through the hymnbook, I see many hymns are being edited into more modern English.

Now, sermon time. The preacher is the Rev Dr Tony Martin. Not your average parson, this one. He's been relieving here for a year while the search for a new minister has gone on. A New Zealander initially trained for the Presbyterian ministry, Tony served as a chaplain in the British Army before being seconded to NATO in Germany, where he was appointed senior chaplain, with the rank of Lieutenant-Colonel (local).

Tony's well presented, as you'd expect a senior military officer to be, but in his choice of words, clarity of thought, and passion for the Christian message, he's simply outstanding. He's lived in desperately dangerous warzones; men he's known and counselled personally have been killed or mutilated. You can hear the proverbial pin drop. No mere after-dinner speech, this—there are tears in his eyes and an audible trembling in his voice as he recounts 'being there'.

Technology has arrived here in the Lowburn Chapel. Tony has a 'clicker' to bring up slides on a screen to emphasise key points and show illustrations. Today, he speaks about demons—not the adventure fantasy of 'Angels and Demons', but the real demons that control people's lives: porn, booze, sense of failure, fear of rejection and more. There are touches of humour, some at his own expense, but the intent is clear and thought-provoking.

Too soon, it's over. We sing one more hymn. Such a good fit with what we've just heard . . .

Make me a captive, Lord, and then I shall be free;
Force me to render up my sword, and I shall conqueror be.
I sink in life's alarms, when by myself I stand;
Imprison me within Your arms, and strong shall be my
hand! [66]

Then, as it has been in Christian services for centuries past, it's the benediction. We start as we began—I recognise the last verse of the hymn we sang at the beginning:

All praise and thanks to God who reigns in highest heaven
The Father and the Son and Spirit, now be given;
The one, eternal God whom earth and heaven adore,
For thus it was, is now, and shall be evermore!

Now the organ bursts into life, and we sing the 'Threefold Amen'—another centuries-old tradition. "Amen! Amen! Amen!" Which means, more or less, "So be it! So be it! So be it!" A kind of endorsement of what's gone before.

The organ plays while we all greet each other on the way out. Very informal. I shake the minister's hand, appreciating the warmth of his greeting. Now, there's morning tea available, prepared and served by two more rostered volunteers. Away to our left, people are arriving for the 10:30 am service. I'm told that the intermingling happening for ten to fifteen minutes now is seen as important. "We're one people!" one nine o'clocker insists, "we just have two styles of worship." OK. I resolve to attend the later service soon . . .

---

66 *Make Me A Captive, Lord,* George Matheson, 1890, public domain.

... And so I do. I come to a 10:30 am service the following week. This is in the main auditorium which seats three hundred people, with overflow out into the foyer area where the morning tea is served. The same kind of comfy seats are used as in the Lowburn Chapel for the 9 am event. The flexible auditorium is set up by church volunteers for both weekday renters and large church gatherings, primarily held on Sundays. As I enter, it's nice to be recognised by a couple of people I'd met the previous week. Not hard to be a visitor here.

After a brief welcome, the service starts with a group of musicians on stage facing us. A large cross hangs in the centre of the wall behind them. Song lyrics are displayed on big screens to the left and right of the stage. The musicians lead us in songs that are in very informal modern English. These songs seem almost conversational with God. Themes include His goodness and faithfulness through good times and bad.[67]

I count sixty-seven people here today, roughly double last week's nine o'clock turnout. There are around ten primary school-aged children and many more women than men. I recognise two couples from the 9 am service. This congregation includes a wider age range and more diverse representation from people of the Pacific islands, Asia, the Middle East, South Africa, Europe, the UK, and South America.[68]

This really is a production, staffed by various volunteers: the music team on stage, a sound and visuals team in a little booth at the back, greeters at the door, the elder leading, someone

---

67   *Goodness of God,* Jenn Johnson, Bethel Music, 2019.

68   Sunday School numbers are higher in school term time. Children go out to Sunday School in term time, and sometimes, in holiday time when a progamme for them has been arranged

offering prayers and someone else doing Bible readings. It's Tony preaching again today and it's all noticeably family-friendly; small children come and go to the bathroom or to the kitchen for a glass of water. Notices are much the same as in the earlier service, with evidence of the church's efforts to be a supportive community. One older lady (from the 9 am) is asking for muscular men to help with a change of carpet in her home! The 'Celebrations' part arrives—yes, chocolates are on offer as they were in the earlier event! A local school teacher earns (a) a chocolate of her choice; (b) applause (c) the on-stage band striking up 'Happy Birthday' and everyone singing.

The children go out to Sunday School. The musicians lead us in a second bracket of songs. Same direct-chat-with-God style. Most stand while these songs are sung. Key lyrics are often repeated, so the song takes longer, and some older people stay seated. No one seems to mind. You don't have to stand—you don't have to sing if you don't want to. No one is on show here.

Now, while we still remain standing, the elder leading the service invites us to share anything encouraging from the week past. Someone prays, then another quotes from the Psalms—well-known words that even non-church-goers recognise:

> *I will lift up my eyes unto the hills. Where does my help come*
> *from? From the Lord, who made heaven and earth!*
> *Psalm 121:1-2*

We sing one last song, and then Jim Harrington leads us in prayer. His compassion for those for whom he prays is obvious: the elderly, orphans, broken families, single parents, refugees, oppressed countries, and more. Jim then reminds us all that God does not want any to perish: "With You, O Lord, there are no lost causes." A former missionary himself,[69] Jim prays for people in all the countries in which those from this church have served (or are about to serve) as missionaries—Thailand, Burkina Faso (West Africa), Zambia, Malawi, Hungary, Nepal . . . quite a list. I wonder if this church is unique in this global focus. Jim ends voicing the hope that "this church shines as the Light of Christ."

Married or single, everyone is part of the family, embraced so warmly that some, like Duncan, are keen to be with church family and attend worship twice in the same morning.

Tony begins his sermon fifty minutes after the 10:30 am start. The subject is 'The Last Day of a Man of God' and recounts the story of Elijah and Elisha, religious leaders from the Old Testament (2 Kings 2). The sermon is about the last day in the life of the older man, Elijah. Not a story that even hard-nosed modern men and women will manage easily. Tony challenges us all to be sure to finish our lives well, as Elijah does here . . . and to remember that none of us knows when the end of our life might come.

He also urges us not to be like the school of fifty prophets who came to watch but didn't want to be involved. No useful contribution from them! We need to be participants, not mere spectators.

I'm fascinated by the 'Chariots of Fire' bit and have seen the movie by the same name more than once.[70] But what captures my attention now is the supernatural nature of the story:

---

69   Jim and Helen Harrington were missionaries in Burkina Faso, West Africa. See Chapters 6 and 11 for detailed coverage of missionary efforts related to CPC.

70   *Chariots of Fire* is a 1981 Warner Bros movie directed by Hugh Hudson.

As they were walking along and talking together, suddenly a chariot of fire and horses of fire appeared and separated the two of them, and Elijah went up to heaven in a whirlwind. Elisha saw this and cried out, "My father! My father! The chariots and horsemen of Israel!" And Elisha saw him no more.

2 Kings 2:11-12 NIV

Even in this age of rockets to the moon, we humans have our limits. God sees to it that, like Eric Liddell in the movie, the two stars of the Old Testament story—Elijah, the old campaigner and Elisha, the heir apparent—are seen as untouchables. This is God in control of the world Christians believe He has made. Powerful stuff, and a real challenge to secular men and women who think everything is explainable in human terms.

Cromwell had just experienced Tony's last sermon, a thirty-six-minute address. No sign of boredom here. I'm glad I've been in on this, and more than a little thoughtful as I depart.

The Church Today

Marie Stiven rolling up her sleeves

Christine and Ross Hansen, Les Wickham, Ted Mallett

Alpha Course participants, 2019

Running the race

Sunday evening
11th August
@ Cromwell Presbyterian
5—7pm
Everyone is welcome

Enquiries to:
Marie 03 445 1814
Jan 021 040 8671

Koha/donations welcome—
includes a light meal

To book: email office@cromchurch.co.nz

RSVP by Wednesday, 7 August for catering

Messy Church

Barbara Carston,
Session Clerk, 2019

The Light Party

Jan Stanton and Carol
Wickham with the littlies

Walk of the Cross,
Easter 2019

Two-Course Tuesday, 2021
Tom Landreth aged 101 on the left

Wednesday Study
Group outing, 2024

George and Bette Clearwater

Bill and Noreen How-John

Leen and Anne du Mez

Kate and Lindsay Borrie

Nicola Clark, Church Administrator

James Watt, Synod Moderator and Rev Reece Frith

CHAPTER FOURTEEN

Some of the Continuity People

MOST ORGANISATIONS HAVE THEIR GO-TO PEOPLE, don't they? Think of these people as the oil that keeps things happening, or rocks to be depended on in tough times. Some of the CPC people who belong in this category are talked about elsewhere in this book, but in this chapter, we celebrate others.

Christine Hansen has been in office here for yonks. In most offices, in fact, since she and her husband, Ross, arrived in Cromwell in the early 70s. She was even Moderator of Synod in 2006-2007. Not everyone gets asked to take on that role. Christine has been an elder, Session Clerk, and treasurer, and when her kids were growing up, she took on roles that enabled her to keep an eye on what they were doing—first as a Sunday School teacher, then superintendent, then youth group leader. And on it goes. She quit as a practising elder because, after thirty years, it was time for someone else to step up. But she's still the go-to person. She certainly hasn't disappeared off the scene.

Christine is also the best large-group cook you could hope for. Today, she's been cooking for Two-Course Tuesday. Sixty-plus hungry mouths getting a fully-cooked lunch for fifteen dollars each. She's organised it, bought the food, prepped the day before, and the kitchen is spotless by the time this is written, three hours after the happy lunch attendees have all gone home satisfied.

Husband Ross does his bit around the church, too. As a former elder and current Board of Managers member, he oversees the church's assets, including the building, its contents, and the manse, which the new minister moved into last week. Ross and Christine owned a motor garage business for years, and they complemented each other well, with Christine running the admin and Ross the workshop. He's a second-mile man, too, always willing to lend a hand. He used to do the Automobile Association call-out service around town and now makes nightly rounds of the church premises, checking doors and windows are locked.

It's hard for Christine to let go and let others. Remember, she's held pretty much every responsible position the church has. She's direct, but not immovable. Sharp elbows? Sometimes, perhaps. But things get moved and shaken—credit where credit's due.

Murray and Kerran Brown came from the Dunedin Church of Christ, and every dyed-in-the-wool Presbyterian should be glad that there isn't a Church of Christ in Cromwell or we might have missed out on their incredible contribution. Read on and see why. Kerran Brown is amazing. How else do you run a family of five when your own health has been dicey for the last forty years? And do not doubt it: the list of Murray's achievements has only been possible because Kerran manages the home front so well and has always been Murray's number-one sounding board.

Murray, like Christine Hansen, has done the hard leadership yards: Session Clerk in the dark days of the Presbytery sacking in 1989, youth group leader, and very significantly, the man who saw through the shift from the old church premises to the new. Things were said to him at that time that shouldn't have been, and there were even anonymous messages left in the Browns' letterbox that hurt them deeply. Never a word of complaint was said publicly by the Browns, nor any reference to the many dollars from their own pockets to help get the new church project over the line.

There's more. Murray has been a stalwart of the Cromwell Rugby Club's scrum, the boss of a real estate company, and has chaired the Cromwell College Board. He's dashed off to Africa to check on daughter Alison, who was doing her bit of missionary service in support of the Harringtons. He's been chair of the CPC Board of Managers. The Browns are in Waimate now, to be closer to family, but have found it hard to live away from Cromwell. Theirs was a huge contribution to church and community life here. They are missed by many. (The author is immensely sad to record here that Murray Brown passed away in the last week of December, 2024).

Another Murray came to live in Cromwell in the late 1970s— Murray Robertson, who was one of the many who joined the Clyde Dam project workforce. Murray and his first wife, Janeice, belonged to the Salvation Army in Dunedin. Both were talented musicians and generous givers of their time to church matters. Sadly, Janeice died of cancer in the early 2000s. Murray has married again—Shirley, who was the receptionist for CPC for several years and often helps in the kitchen now when hospitality is needed. You know that people really care about their church when after so many years in leadership roles, they quietly put themselves on the weekly cleaning roster.

A considerate, gentle and humble fellow, Murray has been sharing his multiple musical talents in the church for nearly fifty years—as singer, guitarist, and mouth organist. These days, he often does a one-man show for the oldies at one or other of the town's two retirement villages. He's been a music leader in the 10:30 am service for many years, but he's also done his bit as an elder and member of the Board of Managers. His practical skills made him a vital member of the volunteer team that went to Thailand in 2013 to help the Potters with the hostel at Mae Chaem.

Then there's Edith Geddis. Originally from Ireland, Edith is a retired medical practitioner who leads the pastoral care part of CPC's life. That doesn't mean the ministers don't do this personal caring for the flock anymore, but it does mean that they have a smaller part than used to be the case up until about 1990. Edith's car can be seen pulled up outside the door of the church before 9 am on any given Sunday and before 10:45 am one Tuesday a month. She either brings the less mobile oldies to church herself or arranges for others to do that. She also makes an effort to visit oldies in person.

Edith is highly articulate; her prayers at 9 am services show her well-informed awareness of people's needs elsewhere in the world, as well as here in New Zealand. From time to time, she has a meeting of CPC people who are doing their bit to help those struggling in the church family. She's something of a visionary, too: as a result of Bible-in-Schools becoming surplus to Goldfields School requirements, Edith has come up with the intriguing possibility of CPC running its own private school, making use of the spaces in the church complex that is currently let out to community users. Crying over spilt milk is not Edith's way. Children must hear the Jesus story one way or another.

Barbara Carston is the current Session Clerk, having taken over from Mervyn Mitchell in 2022. She worked for many years in a commercial accounting role, before turning her main focus to CPC, especially in the long gap between the departure of Douglas Bradley in 2022 and the arrival of Reece Frith in 2024. The Session Clerk at such times is truly a continuity person, and the work can pile up mercilessly. CPC people have much to be thankful to Barbara for.

Paul Johnstone is an able and experienced property developer with an accounting and management background. He's also been chair of the national board of Manna Christian Stores[71]. For six years in the 1990s, he was the lay pastor of a rural Southland Presbyterian parish, which is eighty kilometres from one end—at Kingston, at the south end of Lake Wakatipu—to the other, at Balfour. A talented actor and singer, Paul recently played a lead role in a Central Otago production of the musical *Les Miserables*.

His contribution at CPC has been significant, too. He's been a member of the Ministry Settlement Board for the last two ministers, Bradley and Frith, even though it has meant signing in by Zoom call sometimes when business or family matters have taken him to far-off places. Paul is also an experienced

---

71 A Christian bookstore chain, currently owned by the Bible Society of New Zealand.

and level-headed elder, having previously been in that role in churches in Gore and Invercargill. He's had real health challenges to face, but still, he's upfront as a service leader, recently offering memorable prayers for local, national and world situations. Paul's wife, Jocelyn, is also a capable professional, being an experienced nurse and clinical manager. She too has contributed to church life, playing a significant part in the appointment of Mandi Geustyn in 2017.

Mervyn and Judy Mitchell are another couple who came to Cromwell with vast experience through their involvement in another Presbyterian church. Mervyn was an elder at the Clinton Church for thirty-seven years, and Session Clerk for ten of those years. He became Session Clerk and an elder in Cromwell in 2016. He did a year as a farmer volunteer in the New Hebrides in 1968-1969 and has since worked with short-term teams in the Philippines and Israel. Judy was part of the Israel team too. Both the Mitchells have wrestled with health issues in recent times but are back to something like their old selves at the time of writing.

This is a good time to mention the musicians. The 9 am service follows the traditional pattern used by churches for hundreds of years—an organist up front playing before and after the service and accompanying four hymns during it. Currently, there's a roster of four people who do this. Back in time, Alison Smith was the sole organist for a good few years. She dropped off the roster around 2015, but her influence is still there beside the organ—several old hymnbooks and other Christian music on a shelf adjacent to the organ for use if required.

The 10:30 am Sunday service at CPC is very different from the days when it used to be just the minister up the front, with an organist off to one side. Ann Davis, a newly-appointed elder and another retired medical practitioner, manages the music for this service. Ann is one of the vocalists in the mini-band, and brass music is provided by Myles Garmonsway. The electronics are controlled from a large console at the back, where Peter Townend leads a team providing the expertise. Catherine Forsyth is CPC's top musician nowadays. She has a degree in music from Otago University and shares the leadership of the Music Department at Cromwell College with another talented CPC keyboard player, Trish Copland.

There are so many more who contribute to CPC life. John Thorpe and more recently, Peter Wood have made the church vegetable garden into a plentiful source of food at a time when those less well-off are struggling with food prices. Les Dick is a gifted arranger of flowers, not a gift often ascribed to farmers! Les and his wife, Lyn, are also generous providers of accommodation and food for a wide range of people. Lindsay Borrie has led the Board of Managers capably for many years. Harrington hospitality is legendary, especially for the Wednesday Men's Breakfast and the monthly Fish and Chip night in support of CPC missionary causes. Jan Stanton has given real leadership to Rhythm & Dance, and, more recently, to Messy Church.

Must mention the office people … Nicola it is at present. Nicola did five years of hard work in there, tried to go do something different, and, well it's a long story, but we needed her to come back, and sure enough, she did!

There are of course many others. Volunteers who offer help in the kitchen, quietly prepare food for funerals, lead prayers and/or attend prayer meetings and Bible studies, roster on to do readings in Sunday services, arrange tables and chairs in orderly fashion for the next users, cut the grass, clean, and donate food to the local food bank on a weekly basis.

And finally, a special word for the wives and children of the manse. Always on show. Privacy and space away from the public eye can be hard to find!

CHAPTER FIFTEEN

Twilight Years

THEY ARE A WARM BUNCH, THESE CPC OLDIES. MOST are regulars at the 9 am Sunday service, even though it can be perishing cold getting up for this in the depths of the Central Otago winter.

The 10:45 am start time is a little friendlier for the Evergreens service held on the second Tuesday of the month in the Lowburn Chapel. You don't have to be over seventy-five to attend, but most are. The oldest and least mobile are often picked up and taken home afterwards by people like Edith Geddis, the retired doctor and lead organiser of CPC's pastoral care efforts. Edith is sensible and practical and has a seemingly effective network which usually enables her to find out quickly when someone needs help. Attending the Evergreens service is a good way to stay in contact with each other, given that when you're in your nineties, you don't get out and about to visit people so much.

They don't want special privileges, but they do get well cared for at Evergreens, courtesy of Marie Stiven. A retired teacher like her husband, Alf, Marie originally hails from Taranaki. You'll never hear her talking about how much she does, but this remarkable woman has been an elder for the last twenty years, stalwart of the Monday night prayer meeting, organiser of and preacher at Evergreens and Messy Church services, and likewise at a monthly service at Ripponburn, a nearby rest home. She's also a regular visitor of oldies wherever they are in Cromwell.

As if all that were not enough, Marie is the relief manager at the local op shop, one day a week.[72] Marie does more than a forty-hour week as a volunteer for CPC and is a major contributor to a lot of the church programmes. She runs a quarterly Messy Church—yes, that's what it's called—an informal church gathering, mainly for young families, with a shared meal in the middle of it. Marie also contributed to Bible-in-Schools, but now that has stopped at both the Cromwell primary schools, CPC is implementing other strategies like Messy Church to connect with children.[73]

The organist sings as well as playing at Evergreens. Trevor is relatively young—only in his late seventies—so it kind of suits him to play because he'd be coming anyway, and Gill Salt, another retiree, plays sometimes, too. It's a communion service. The whole event is less formal than the 9 am, which is itself pretty relaxed. People stay seated to sing, and the hymns are time-honoured, such as *Tell Me the Old, Old Story* and *The Old Rugged Cross*. There's also a rewrite of a song known by anyone who ever went to Sunday School:

---

72 Helen Harrington, the returned missionary whose efforts in West Africa we tracked in Chapter 6, is the boss at this op-shop.
73 Readers may recall that Mandi, featured in Chapter 12, works promoting this programme around Presbyterian churches.

Jesus loves me, this I know
Though my hair is white as snow
Though my sight is growing dim
Still He bids me trust in Him.

It's a shorter service than the Sunday ones. Afterwards, those present are happy to adjourn for a cup of tea and a sandwich or something sweet. Yes, Marie arranges it, and most people stay for fifteen to twenty minutes or more for a good natter. Regulars in this group include Anne and Gordon Gates, pushing ninety now, and contemplating a shift into one or other of the villages. Bette Clearwater, a former nurse widowed some years ago, is there too. She's almost ninety-one but independent, still buzzing around Cromwell in her little car and doing Bible readings in the 9 am service. Marion Burrow came from Owaka in the Catlins area more than fifty years ago for her husband, Russell, to become postmaster. She and Bette are old friends, true Cromwell locals. Another local is Roey Cowie, a mother of nine and well into her nineties. Roey is a resident at Ripponburn. Her trademark smile is never far away.

Ted and Bev Corry, originally Salvation Army, have also been well over thirty years at CPC. How enriched the CPC congregation has been by the input of so many who've come from other traditions! Ted has written a book about his service in the British Merchant Navy. We chat often about epic stories of the sea, such as the Titanic disaster and Nicholas Monsarrat's novel *The Cruel Sea*. Ted is one of the organisers at the local Euchre card-playing group, and he's done his bit for Neighbourhood Watch which keeps an eye on the town during the hours of darkness.

The CPC demographic now includes significant numbers of retirees. Lindsay Borrie, for the past eighteen years on the Board of Managers and not that far off retiring himself, says these oldies are a real strength at CPC because they contribute so much: their presence, their smiling faces (in most cases), financial support, and their institutional knowledge—they're a major source of information for the writing of this book, for example.

People live longer now … plenty of CPC's oldies have reached their nineties and a few, like Elsie McIvor and Tom Landreth, made it well past one hundred and received the coveted letter from the Queen. Programmes at CPC have evolved to cater for retirees with Two-Course Tuesday—the fifteen-dollar slap-up lunch on Tuesdays for any who care to put their names down, Monday aerobics for oldies, and Indoor Bowls in the winter. There's also Care and Friendship, a sort of parallel programme to Two-Course Tuesday which is run by the Anglicans and offers music, recreational activities, and a midday meal.

The two Rest Homes in Cromwell—both now owned by one North Island company—have a good number of CPC oldies amongst their residents. Well into her nineties, Anne du Mez is one of these at Golden View, the newer of the two homes. Several years ago, Anne lost her husband, Leen, a CPC elder for many years. They came out separately from Holland after WWII, met and married in Southland, brought up family, and then retired to Cromwell around the turn of the century. Anne struggles with mobility, but she's as sharp as a tack and keeps the staff at Golden View on their toes. Leen's prayers in church services were legendary. A tall man losing some mobility in his later years, he'd come up to the front slowly, turn and eye the congregation meaningfully, and then say with dignity, "Shall we pray together?" You never doubted Leen's prayers were from the heart.

Others living independently include two of the couples who were elders at the time of the David Caldwell baptism controversy, thirty-five years ago now. Bill How-John was—and is—something of an institution in Cromwell. He ran a painting business for over forty years until his son, William, took over when Bill retired. Bill and Noreen left the Presbyterian Church to attend the New Life Church. They were brave enough—this is a small town, remember—to come back again twenty years later. Talking about their lives with them is memorable for several reasons. They say openly that their marriage survives because of their faith in Jesus Christ; He gave them both the lasting will and ability to love and forgive. They laugh about their cat deserting them to become Rev Doug Stout's spoilt moggy. Noreen's warm impulsiveness comes across as both a strength and a liability. On one unforgettable occasion, she painted over Masonic images in the stained-glass windows that now adorn the Lowburn Chapel. Bill loved the fellowship of the Lodge but left many years ago.

Allan and Sandra Perks, both salt-of-the-earth, long-serving elders, are parents of three delightful children, who like so many others, long ago departed from Cromwell's quiet precinct to see the world. Like Bill and Noreen in the previous paragraph, Allan and Sandra were part of the Session summarily dismissed by Central Otago Presbytery in 1989. It still saddens and disappoints them. They hope for a renewal and building-up of CPC's pastoral care network, especially with the proportion of retirees steadily growing. They aren't that mobile, so they're grateful for former minister Alan Missen who brings them communion whenever he's in Cromwell visiting his daughter, Penny. They struggle, as do many others, to understand why modern ministers don't rate visiting their congregation as an essential—as it was in days past. Rumour has it that the new minister, Reece Frith, is already getting around to see people . . .

Glenda Clarke brought her husband, Garry, to Cromwell, mainly to care for her ageing mother, Elsie. Glenda's dad, Stan McIvor, was a farmer and much-loved elder in the 70s and 80s and came out of retirement to be part of the Interim Session in 1990. Like so many others associated with CPC, Glenda and Garry came from a different denomination, having met and married in an Auckland New Life congregation. Garry is the unusual combination of ordained minister and meteorologist. Those skill sets have taken them to unusual places: the Cook Islands as weatherman and the Chatham Islands as New Life minister! When Elsie died at one hundred and two years of age, they returned to New Life but look back fondly on their connection with CPC. Garry preached often at CPC in the gaps between ministers, and his down-to-earth approach to faith was much appreciated.

THIS CHAPTER CAN'T BE FINISHED WITHOUT recalling a few oldies not with us anymore. We won't see the likes of Ted Mallett again. His passing marked the end of an era. Ted died at ninety-five years of age, just a matter of weeks before this part of the story was written. He had more than his share of the harder side of life. Not long after WWII, he was helping another man on an isolated gold claim when a wall of gravel collapsed. Unspeakable trauma . . . Ted went for help, but the other man died before he could be rescued.

A quiet but resolute man, Ted was treasurer of CPC for forty years. His handwritten financial records were a source of astonishment to modern accountants. During the 1930s Depression, he was brought up in a rock cottage in the Kawarau Gorge where his father worked gold claims and shot rabbits for cash and to feed his family. Ted's wife, Ida, was appointed an elder in 1958. When she passed away somewhat prematurely, an electronic organ was donated by the Mallett family in her memory. It is still in use in the Lowburn Chapel. For a forty-three-year-old instrument, it is in remarkably good condition.

Jim Woods was a soldier in the North African desert in WWII. Jim's wife, Tui, predeceased him by a good number of years, but Jim remained cheerful well into his nineties, his trademark smile never far away. Thinking of Jim makes a natural link to jovial ex-army padre Frank Glen who was part of the church until he died . . . and if we do a mental reset from military to non-military service, how about Harold and Audrey Searle, who were thirty-six years as missionaries in Bolivia, where Harold's parents had already served a similar length of time. What a commitment by one family to people so far from New Zealand!

Marj Bateman, who with her husband, Arnold, worked very hard for years to make a go of their carpet business, kept contributing to CPC after he passed away, as she always had. Illness made Arnold's last years really tough for them both. Marj did the hard yards caring for him.

There are so many more good CPC people whose story is worth telling . . . but we have to stop somewhere. Faith is the common thread, as is a real awareness of the need to sustain the work of the church and to find ways to keep it in front of an increasingly secular population.

Post Script

I WRITE NOW AS ONE WITH A GREAT AFFECTION FOR this church and for the wider Cromwell community. And—in case you've had any doubt as you've read this book—yes, I'm one of those who swims against the cultural tide. I'm a convinced Christian. Jesus of Nazareth is the only hope I can find for a terminally ill world.

It's time to put behind us the disappointments of the past, if we haven't already. That's just part of the baggage that slips off our shoulders when we become Christians.

Together, we look forward to a future that is:

Not about the label but the substance. As a church, we are passionate about people in and around Cromwell following Jesus and genuinely, actively caring for each other and for those around them.

Open to re-shaping tomorrow's church. The prophet Isaiah wrote: *"See, I am doing a new thing! Now it springs up; do you not perceive it? I am making a way in the wilderness and streams in the wasteland"* (Isaiah 43:19,NIV). God wants His church to find new ways forward, so it's great to see new leaders coming through. In 2024, we have a younger and more ethnically diverse set, including elders and managers from the Pacific, the United Kingdom and South Africa.

Aware of the need to re-order priorities. Work and family will still matter but won't be all-consuming. *"I did not come to bring peace, but a sword. For I have come to turn a man against his father, a daughter against her mother, a daughter-in-law against her mother-in-law. A man's enemies will be the members of his own household"* (Matthew 10:34-36). These profoundly upsetting words of Jesus remind us that while we should truly love our families, it's God who tells us in the Bible how we should live. As the English writer JB Phillips insisted more than seventy years ago, our God is too small if we just fit Him in and do His work only if and when there's room in our busy lives to allow it.[74]

Characterised by loving our fellow church members unconditionally. Wow! Jesus said, *"Because you love one another, everyone shall know that you are my disciples"* (John 13:35). Home and study groups ... progressive meals ... camps and church trips ... sharing the big tasks like helping people shift house ... We know that if we let this kind of sharing fade away, the church will be at risk.

Committed to putting the children and young people first. The combination of the scrapping of Bible-in-Schools, and the secular takeover of Sundays

---

74 JB Philips *Your God is too Small*, Epworth Press, London, 1952

for recreational purposes, means that only a small proportion of children have access to the Christian faith nowadays. Annual events like the Light Party and Santa Land help. If you're not a church person, surely you want your children to have the strong moral and ethical values they'll learn at Kids Church and the Youth Group?

Focussed on getting the men back. Yvonne Wilkie was right to note that, "Our theologies are drawn from cultural mores as much as from scripture and church traditions."[75] Men used to make all the rules in secular society as well as in church life, and women were told where they fitted in. A lot has changed, and rightly so. Women are well represented in church leadership now, as indeed they are in secular life—we've had women prime ministers, governors-general, chief justices, and more.

But has the pendulum swung too far? Have men gone off to sulk out of sight? Returned missionary Jim Harrington makes a huge effort to keep men involved in church life, organising men's hunting and shooting weekends, men's breakfasts with invited speakers, and also, for quite a few years now, a weekly 6 am men's breakfast.

Is the outnumbering of men in church activities mostly just men choosing to defer to women? It's not desirable

75 Yvonne Wilkie, *Weaving Vision, Heritage and Hope: 150 Years of the Presbyterian Synod of Otago and Southland,* 1866-2016 p155

that men struggle with being led by women in church, but sometimes, they do.

Reece Frith offers another angle: men find it harder than women to admit that they're not self-sufficient, that they need the sustaining love of God in their lives, His comfort in times of loss, His grace to help them deal with conflict in their lives. It's a season in the journey of the church, says Reece. Capturing the young men is key, as is working in small groups. It seems certain this is already a work in progress.

There *is* slippage in the number of men attending. Male role models for young people are essential. We'll need new strategies to keep the men on board.

Visible in New Zealand Society. The Christian faith must re-assert its place in New Zealand society. Rob Pendreigh was right to be concerned, soon after he became minister at Balclutha Presbyterian Church, when the group of dignitaries invited to be on the podium when the new town hall was opened didn't include any Christian minister.

While the church remains strong, one would be forgiven for thinking that Christian heritage has all but vanished from civic life in New Zealand. We will need to be intentional if we are to have a voice into whatever the community is doing. It will take a concerted effort to be properly visible in New Zealand society.

THE LAST WORD IN THIS BOOK BELONGS TO REECE
Frith, who begins service as Minister of Cromwell Presbyterian
Church in mid-2024. He and his wife Kay are inducted on the
afternoon of Sunday 28 July. About 120 of us are welcomed by
Cromwell's own James Watt, Moderator of Southern Presbytery,
who observes that "It's good for us Southern Presbyterians to
have light and sun on our backs." Literally and figuratively true,
that is. People present are wearing everything from bush shirts to
academic robes. Reece himself is in suit and tie. Must be a special
occasion, because he prefers more relaxed clothing.

As Presbyterian ministers have for more than a hundred years,
Reece reads 'The Formula' aloud,[76] then signs it to indicate he
will abide by it. The event closes with a procession of locals
who present Kay and Reece with items that symbolise their new
location, such as: a Highlanders flag, a map of the south, a scarf,
and even bottled cherries.

Four months later, Reece and the author chat in Reece's study.
He and Kay and their three children, Tayla, Conrad and Pippa,
have settled well. Reece speaks of the 'good signs of life and hope'
he's experienced so far. Every church has its own culture. God
has been faithful to CPC in the past, in good times and bad. He
likes that most church people have strong connections into the
community. People are getting used to his style of preaching, too;
he uses a microphone because his preaching voice is quieter than

---

76 *The Formula:* A solemn declaration that ministers and elders make when they
are first ordained or when they take up a new position. The formula includes
promises to uphold the church's doctrines and to fulfill their duties.

some. He also stops mid-sermon and asks people to talk about points he's been raising. Yes, new for CPC, but why not?

Reece puts it well: God has His plans and purposes, and they won't be put aside if we are true to Him. It's good that this week he's been off on a tramping trip with other Central Otago ministers. Being part of a team is important.

As we finish our chat, compliments about Reece's efforts to visit people are shared. "Whenever I can," he says. *An excuse offered in advance?* This man does seem full of quiet intent.

PEOPLE IN CROMWELL PRESBYTERIAN CHURCH WILL go on. They've survived their own mess-ups by the grace of God. No doubt, there'll be more crises to face around the next bend in the road. They're not perfect—far from it—but there's a strong sense that God is amongst them, and that His grace is sufficient for every need and every new challenge.

There's hope, truckloads of it, for the future. Christians call it the 'resurrection hope'—madness to humanistic, secular folks, but light and life to Christians. 'Strength for today, and bright hope for tomorrow,' wrote Thomas Chisholm.[77] That God-given strength is still available today, and so is that bright hope, whatever our tomorrows might bring.

Be sure of it: this church has no plans to quit.

---

77 From Tom Chisholm's hymn *Great is Thy Faithfulness*, public domain.

The Current Cromwell Session

Stewart Bolger

Barbara Carston (Session Clerk)

Ann Davis

Rev. Reece Frith

Sandra Hunter

Paul Johnstone

Linda Lamb

Ann-Marie Leyser (Retired, 2024)

Aisea Ma

Mervyn Mitchell

Marie Stiven (Retired, 2024)

Acknowledgements

To the late Cathy Mann, whose enthusiasm for this project was unwavering right up to the time of her passing in early December 2024. She provided much background information, several stories, a book about the Arrowtown Church, and many photographs.

To Barbara Carston, Session Clerk for CPC, whose own work commitments and her church workload meant she didn't need this project at all. She has provided books as background information.

To Christine Hansen, long-standing leader at CPC, who took the risk and approached me to write this book and offered help in whatever ways she could.

To the staff of the Presbyterian Centre at the Hewitson Library, Knox College, who made me at home when I came to access information from such resources there which they were allowed to let me see.

To the fifty-six people I have 'interviewed'. You have trusted me with what has sometimes been quite sensitive information. I have tried very hard not to betray confidences or to let you down in any other way. In particular, I thank those who are not practising Christians or regular churchgoers, but whose perspective has been invaluable.

To Tony Martin, who was the Stated Supply Minister at CPC for a year. Tony is an author and brought that experience to our CPC publishing committee. He has generously acted as editor and sounding board for me as I encountered some of the thorny issues CPC has had to deal with over the years. As if all that were not enough, he very kindly wrote the foreword for this book.

To Alan Missen, who provided me with photographs, books about the earliest days of Presbyterianism in Otago and Southland, and other insights.

To the Hocken Library at the University of Otago for such prompt replies to questions asked.

To Reece Frith, Cromwell's minister as we head into year 151; we all wish him well as he leads us on the uphill climb.

To Anya and Jeff McKee and the team at Torn Curtain Publishing who have been encouraging throughout the process. There'd be no book without them.

And most of all, to my wife Jackie, who has had to put up with this enormous ten-month intrusion into our lives and the unsettling effects this intrusion has had on me. Fifty-five years of Trevor McKinlay is a long sentence!

Cromwell Parish Ministers 1875–2025

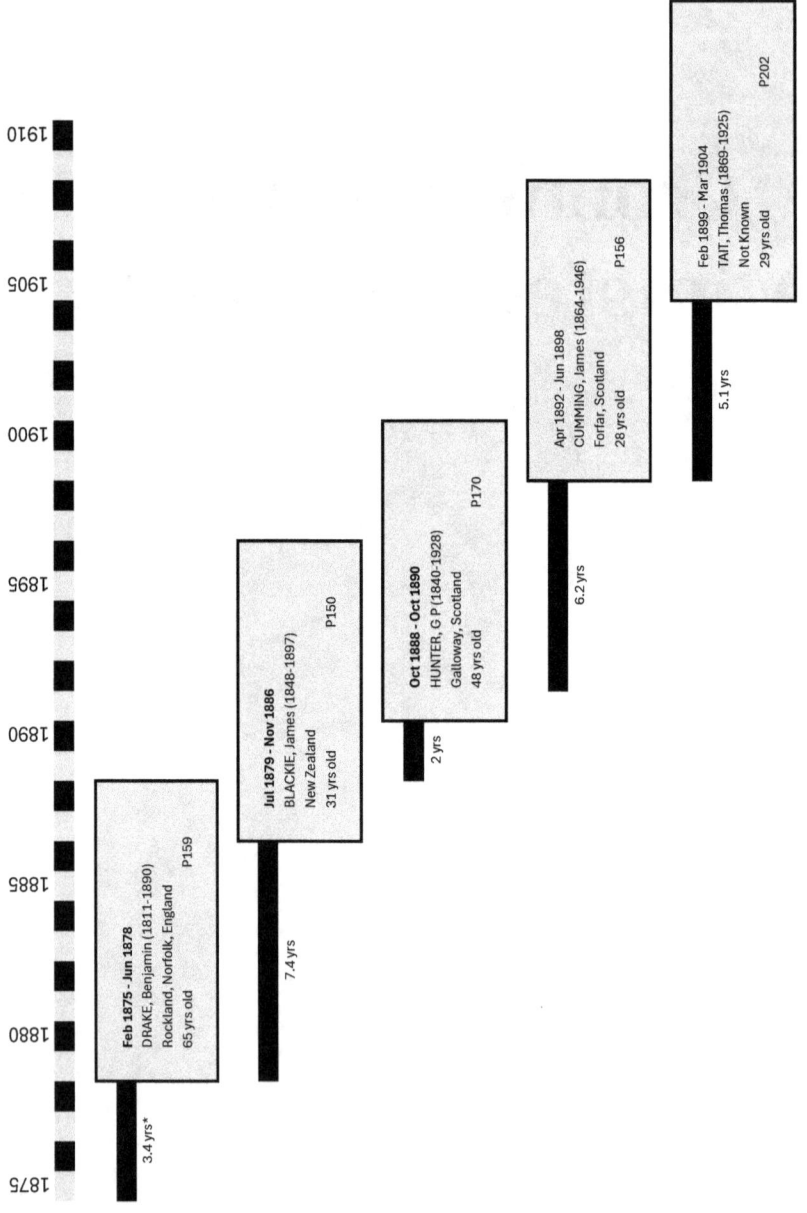

Feb 1875 - Jun 1878
DRAKE, Benjamin (1811-1890)
Rockland, Norfolk, England
65 yrs old
P159

3.4 yrs*

Jul 1879 - Nov 1886
BLACKIE, James (1848-1897)
New Zealand
31 yrs old
P150

7.4 yrs

Oct 1888 - Oct 1890
HUNTER, G P (1840-1928)
Galloway, Scotland
48 yrs old
P170

2 yrs

Apr 1892 - Jun 1898
CUMMING, James (1864-1946)
Forfar, Scotland
28 yrs old
P156

6.2 yrs

Feb 1899 - Mar 1904
TAIT, Thomas (1869-1925)
Not Known
29 yrs old
P202

5.1 yrs

1875 1880 1885 1890 1895 1900 1905 1910

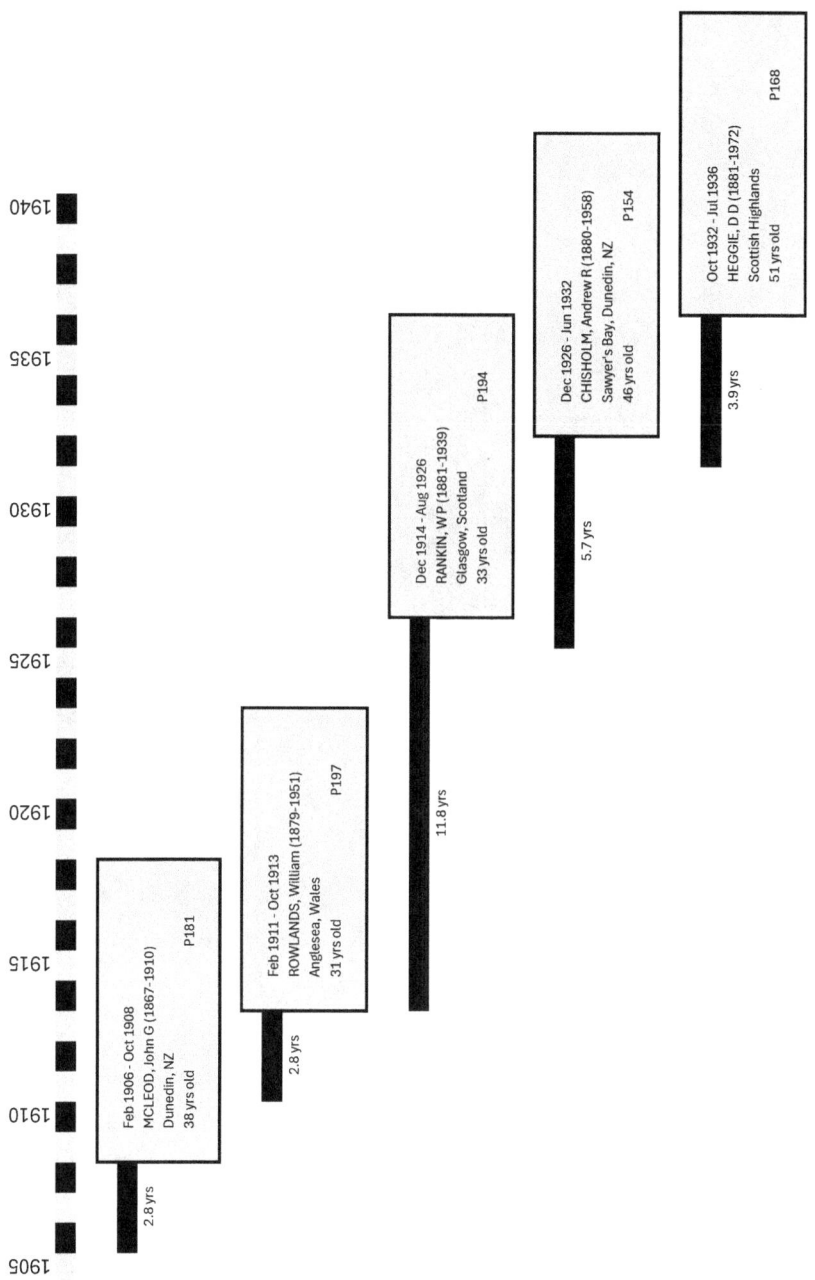

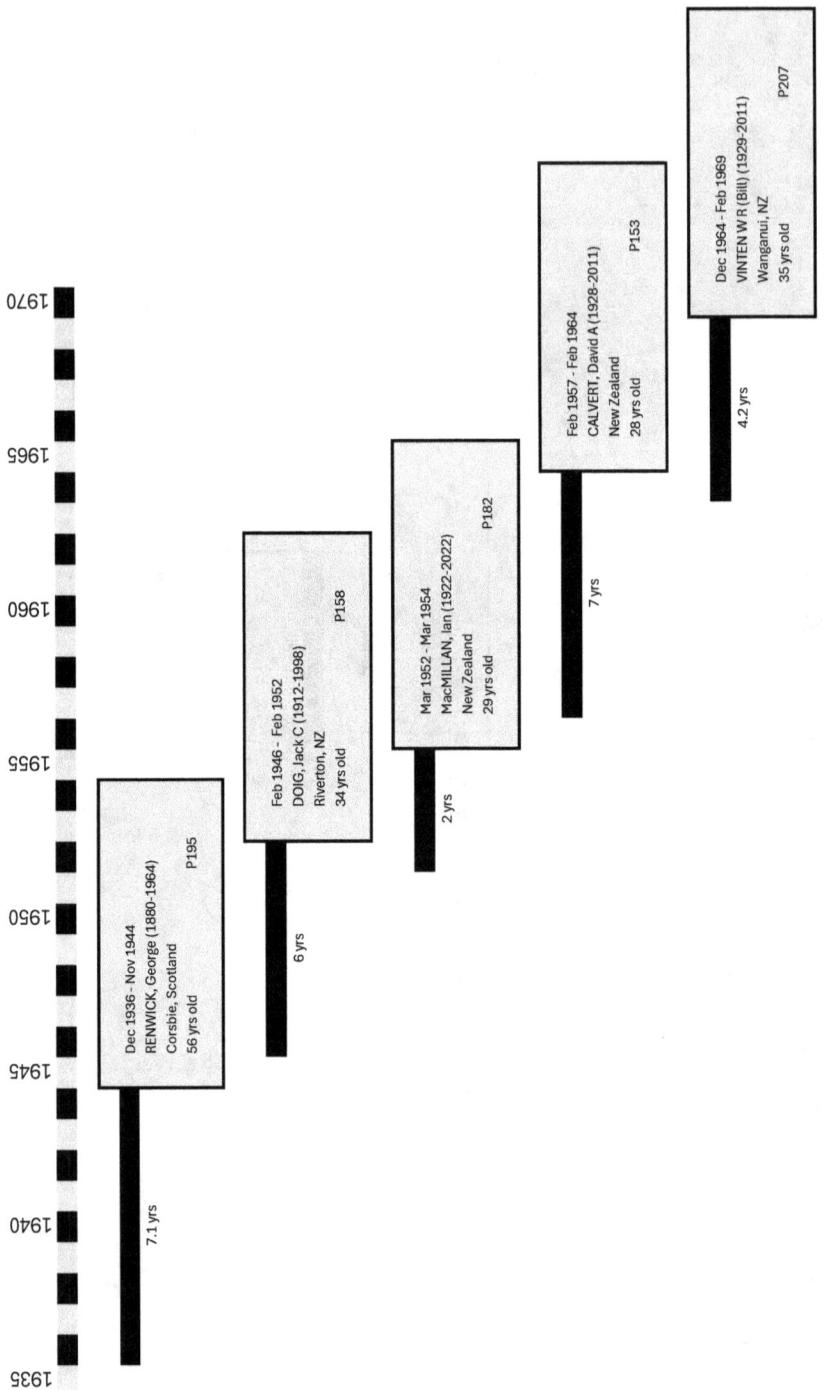

Dec 1936 - Nov 1944
RENWICK, George (1880-1964)
Corsbie, Scotland
56 yrs old
P195

7.1 yrs

Feb 1946 - Feb 1952
DOIG, Jack C (1912-1998)
Riverton, NZ
34 yrs old
P158

6 yrs

Mar 1952 - Mar 1954
MacMILLAN, Ian (1922-2022)
New Zealand
29 yrs old
P182

2 yrs

Feb 1957 - Feb 1964
CALVERT, David A (1928-2011)
New Zealand
28 yrs old
P153

7 yrs

Dec 1964 - Feb 1969
VINTEN W R (Bill) (1929-2011)
Wanganui, NZ
35 yrs old
P207

4.2 yrs

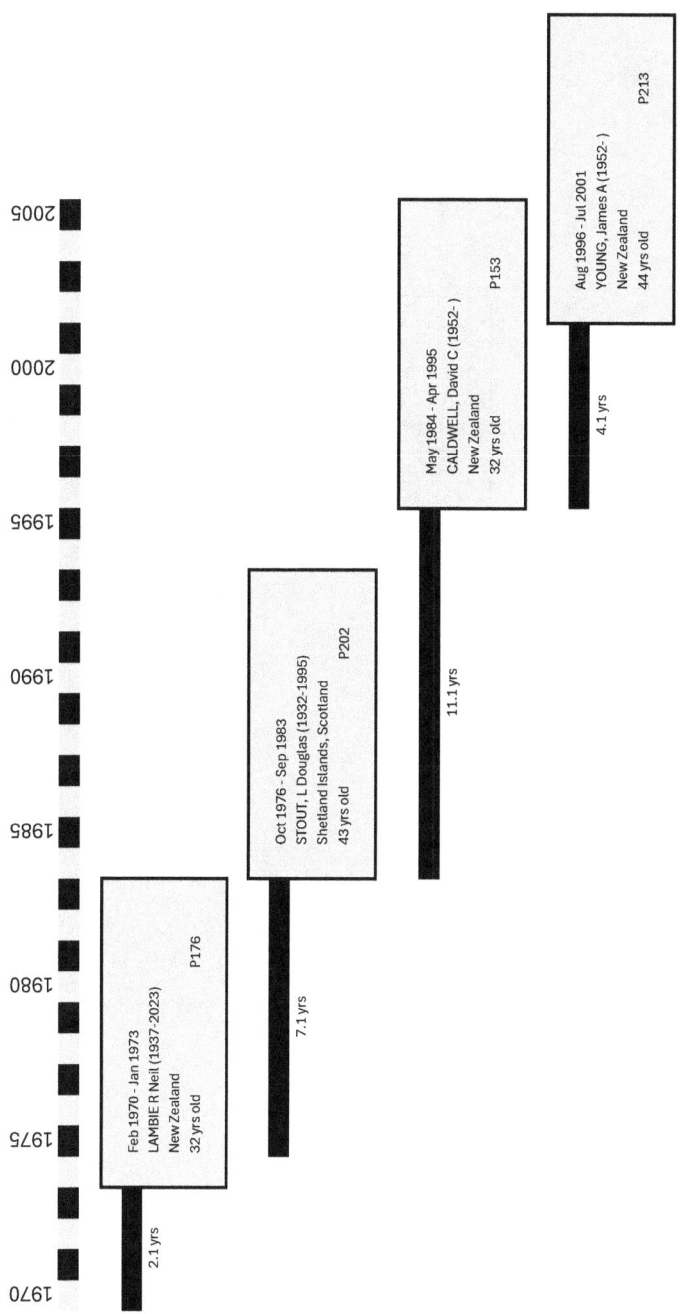

Feb 1970 - Jan 1973
LAMBIE R Neil (1937-2023)
New Zealand
32 yrs old
P176

2.1 yrs

Oct 1976 - Sep 1983
STOUT, L Douglas (1932-1995)
Shetland Islands, Scotland
43 yrs old
P202

7.1 yrs

May 1984 - Apr 1995
CALDWELL, David C (1952-)
New Zealand
32 yrs old
P153

11.1 yrs

Aug 1996 - Jul 2001
YOUNG, James A (1952-)
New Zealand
44 yrs old
P213

4.1 yrs

2005
2000
1995
1990
1985
1980
1975
1970

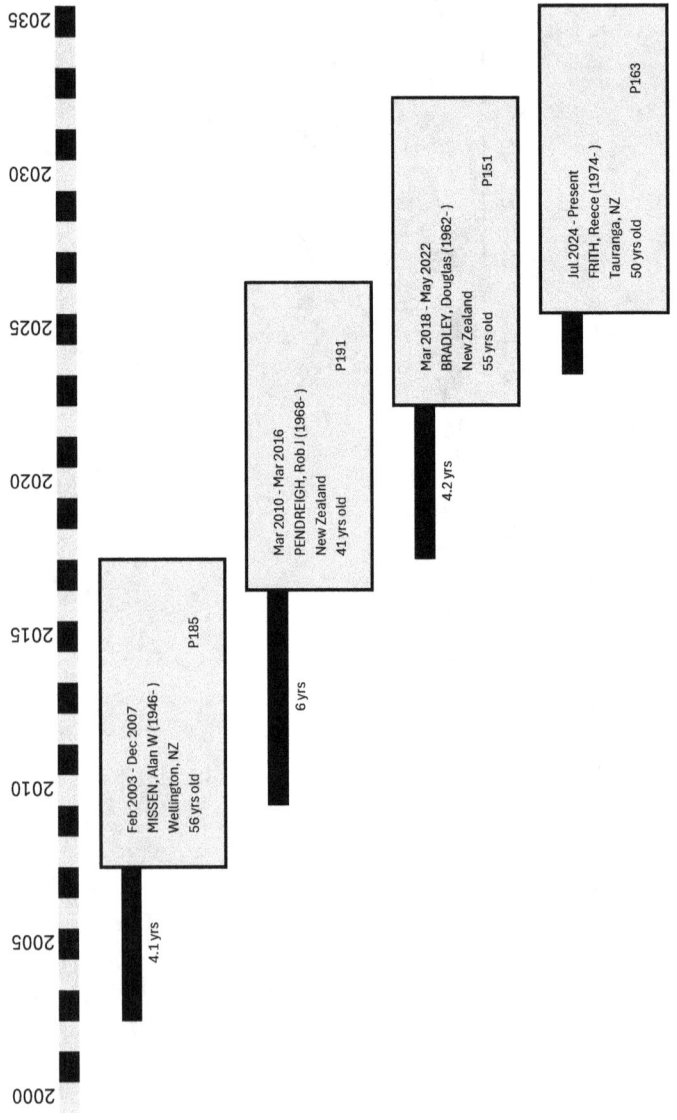

Feb 2003 - Dec 2007
MISSEN, Alan W (1946-)
Wellington, NZ
56 yrs old

P185

4.1 yrs

Mar 2010 - Mar 2016
PENDREIGH, Rob J (1968-)
New Zealand
41 yrs old

P191

6 yrs

Mar 2018 - May 2022
BRADLEY, Douglas (1962-)
New Zealand
55 yrs old

P151

4.2 yrs

Jul 2024 - Present
FRITH, Reece (1974-)
Tauranga, NZ
50 yrs old

P163

* Though not recognised as 'Presbyterian' by the Presbytery of the day, the Rev Ben Drake, Cromwell's first minister, served more than six years as the de facto minister before being officially accredited and inducted in February 1875.

The twenty-two completed ministries have averaged 5 years 5 months. In round numbers, this means the church has had a fully-contracted, 'inducted' minister for four years out of every five.

Longevity: Rev Ian MacMillan, the equal shortest-serving minister, (2yrs 0 mths) lived to the oldest age! (99 years and 10 months). His wife Myrie also lived a long life, passing just four days short of her ninety-fourth birthday.

Rev MacMillan was one of only two who married while 'in office'. The other was Rev Dr Cumming.

Only one minister in the last eighty years was born outside New Zealand—Rev Doug Stout.

NB: In each case, PXXX denotes their reference in the Presbyterian Ministers' Register.

Members and Adherents Serving Overseas

CROMWELL PRESBYTERIAN CHURCH MEMBERS AND ADHERENTS
serving in mission/volunteer roles overseas (for periods of six months or more)

Name(s)	Dates o/seas	Agency	Role
Trevor McKinlay	Feb–Dec 1964	VSA	Teacher, A'ana District School, Upolu, Western Samoa
Beryl Anderson, nee Beaton with spouse Doug Anderson	July 64–Dec 65 1968-77 1977-81	Pres OMB Pres OMB Pres OMB	Nurse, Vaemali Hospital, Epi, New Hebrides Spouse was Lecturer/Pastor, Singapore Spouse was Pastor, Kuala Lumpur, Malaysia
Harold & Audrey Searle	1966-2002	BIM	Evangelism/practical aid, Bolivia, South America
Mervyn Mitchell	Apr 68 – Apr 69	Pres OMB	Farming, Navota farm, New Hebrides
Libby Smith, nee Sutton	1970-1973	Pres OMB	Nurse, New Hebrides
Alastair & Jacquie Smales	1975-82	OMF	Pastor and lecturer, Indonesia

Name	Years	Pres OMB	Activity
Robert Paterson	1976-1999		Lecturer in Old Testament, Indonesia
Mervyn & Judy Mitchell	Mar 84-Oct 84	YWAM	Youth With A Mission outreach in Philipines
Jim & Helen Harrington	1991-2003	SIM	Church planting /Evangelism /practical aid Djibo, Burkina Faso, West Africa
Alan & Yvonne Wilkinson	1995 ff	Private	Myanmar. Building, Early Years education, evangelism.
Alison Brown	1996	SIM	Teacher for Harrington children, Burkina Faso
Malcolm & Sandy Potter	2001-2022	World Outreach	Young people's ministries, Chiangmai, Northern Thailand
Jim & Diane Young	2003-2018	SIM	Evangelism and medical aid, Malawi
Clarissa Bochel	2005-2019	Private	Ministry to Women & Children, Cambodia & Thailand
Alan & Edith Buxton	2007-2015	Private	Infrastructure projects, Vanuatu
Pete & Christine Johnstone	2013-2020	SIM	Church Planting, evangelism: Burkina Faso & Niger, West Africa

Andrew Buxton Liz Buxton	2007-2014 2008-2014 2009-2014	SIM EngMinInt SIM	Ethiopia (2007) Sudan (2008-14) Uganda (2008) Sudan (2009-14) (Both working in Field Support/Admin)
Daniel & Anita Muir	2015-2023	SIM	Youth Evangelism, Botswana (2015-17); Zambia (2018-23)
Alastair & Krisztina Hansen	2019-2024	OM	Ministry through sport, Hungary
Tim & Sarah Mueller	2024-		South East Asia